Birding Guide to North-East Scotland

including part of the Cairngorms National Park

Mark Sullivan and Ian Francis

RSPB Scotland
Aberdeen and District Local Group
celebrating 40 years

March 2015

This publication should be cited as:

Sullivan, M. and Francis, I.

Birding Guide to North-East Scotland

RSPB Scotland - Aberdeen and District Local Group

First published in 2015 by Pica Design, Aboyne

ISBN 978-0-9561126-7-5

Any profits from the sale of this book will be held by the Aberdeen and District RSPB Local Group for conservation projects in North-East Scotland.

The Royal Society for the Protection of Birds (RSPB) is a registered charity: England and Wales no. 207076, Scotland no. SC037654

http://www.rspb.org.uk/whatwedo/scotland/

Printed and bound by Langstane Press Ltd., Aberdeen

Contents

Introduction

This book started life as an update of two Birding Scotland articles from 2001 and 2002 (Birding Scotland 4/4 & 5/1), and the 1989 Aberdeen and District RSPB Members' Group's "Where to Watch for Birds in and around Aberdeen", produced to mark the centenary of the RSPB. It was felt that the area was poorly served by existing available publications and that the wealth of wildlife sites merited a dedicated treatment.

North-East Scotland is an area often overlooked by birdwatchers. Many travel to the well-known "honey-pots" such as Speyside, the North-West Highlands or the various island groups, without venturing eastward, or only pass through the area on the way to Shetland or Orkney. Even a very brief visit will show the wide range of habitats available, each with its characteristic and sought-after birds. The area covers nearly 7,000km^2, with a coastline of over 170km, and even those living and working in the area may not know some of the more hidden sites.

Over 150 species are known to breed in the area, and regular winter and passage visitors and vagrants bring the total list up to 386 at the end of 2013, with three species awaiting acceptance from 2014 (Spotted Sandpiper, Savi's Warbler and Red-throated Pipit) and one (Harlequin Duck) in January 2015. It is hoped that this guide will give much useful information about where to see birds, and show that an extended visit will allow anyone to encounter a wide range of species. In addition to the birds found here, the area has a great diversity of plants and animals to attract the visiting naturalist. Some examples of these are described below and noted in species accounts.

Acknowledgements

This book would not have been possible without the assistance of many local birders and naturalists who have contributed information to the site descriptions. Paul Baxter (who also contributed the check list), Robert Coleman, John Harrison, Ian Hastie, Ken Shaw, Philip Bloor, Margaret Cowie, Chris Gibbins, Tim Marshall, Stuart Reeves, Andy Webb, Hilary MacBean, John Wills, Nick Williams, Clive McKay, Harry Scott and Bill Craigie are all thanked for their contributions. Hywel Maggs, Nick Littlewood, Paul Baxter, Kirsty Nutt, Jenny Weston, Colin McClean, Shaila Rao, Catriona Reid, Annabel Drysdale, Richard Humpidge, David Welch, Rose Toney, Glenn Roberts, Mick Marquiss and Liz Holden all commented on the various drafts. Many photographers in the area freely provided the pictures for the book, and are listed on page 122. Several photographs are from the estate of Phil Newman, a colleague of Mark Sullivan, who tragically died in 2013, and his wife Debbie is thanked for allowing access to his archive. Special thanks go to Mary Miller for preparing the maps and to Fran Sullivan for formatting and editing the text.

This publication has been produced with the generous support of the Birds of Scotland Fund awarded by the Scottish Ornithologists' Club (SOC) www.the-soc.org.uk, and Aberdeenshire Council's *"Be Part of the Picture"* fund.

The area covered by this guide

In this guide, North-East Scotland comprises the present day local authority areas of Aberdeenshire (6,320km^2) and Aberdeen City (188km^2). It extends from near Montrose in the south, northwards along the coast to Fraserburgh, then west along the north Aberdeenshire and Moray Firth coast to Cullen. Inland, the area covers the catchments of the rivers Deveron, Ythan, Don and Dee, and includes the eastern third of the Cairngorms National Park, extending to the highest tops.

Many of the sites here can be accessed using public transport. For up-to-date bus timetables see: www.stagecoachbus.com/timetable-landing.aspx and www.firstgroup.com/ukbus/aberdeen/journey_planning/timetables.

Public toilet facilities are available: for up-to-date access arrangements see www.aberdeenshire.gov.uk/visit/toilets/ and

www.aberdeencity.gov.uk/planning_environment/environmental/environmental_health/enh_public_toilets.asp.

Access, the law and the wildlife watchers' and photographers' codes

Since legislation in 2003, there has been a legal right of access (non-motorised) to most land and water in Scotland - for going from place to place, for recreation and for education. This is covered fully by the Scottish Outdoor Access Code (see leaflet at www.snh.gov.uk/docs/B621366.pdf), but in essence, access rights revolve around acting responsibly and respecting the interests of other people. For the purposes of this guide, most places can be accessed under these terms. There are some areas which do not fall within access rights and these are usually clear – gardens, buildings and growing crops are examples, and access rights do not extend to using vehicles. It is therefore always crucial to park sensibly and with consideration. Please take into account the reasonable requests of land owners and managers, such as when deer stalking is taking place. The Access Code states that you should not disturb or damage wildlife, and this is reinforced by the birdwatchers' code (www.rspb.org.uk/advice/watchingbirds/code).

Some species are specially protected by law, but in any case the welfare of the species should always come first. In particular, please be aware that damage to breeding birds can be caused by trying to obtain close digital photographs, and habitats can be trampled or disturbed by this. Both are sometimes a serious issue, and there is a growing problem caused by inconsiderate wildlife photographers. All photographers should be aware of good practice in relation to sensitive species, and adhere to the SNH wildlife photographers' code (www.snh.gov.uk/docs/B1080875.pdf).

The wildlife of North-East Scotland can be enjoyed easily and responsibly if these simple guidelines are followed.

A brief guide to habitats and wildlife

North-East Scotland is marked by its richness in birds and bird habitats; many of these are of national or international importance for both breeding and wintering species. The area holds major concentrations of the UK's native pinewoods, coniferous plantations, arctic-alpine uplands, lowland raised bogs, coastal sand dunes and dune heath. Heather moorland, arable farmland and coastal shingle are also well-represented. Many widely-renowned bird sites are covered by this guide: the Cairngorms, Mar Lodge, Lochnagar, Glen Tanar, the Moray Firth, Loch of Strathbeg, the Ythan Estuary and Fowlsheugh. The ornithological richness of North-East Scotland is also illustrated by the fact that the area is second in the UK only to Norfolk in the spring national 24hr bird race competition, with 156 species found by a local birding team on 14th May 2004.

Much of the area is underlain by old, hard rocks, characterised by a succession of stepped relief areas increasing in elevation away from the sea. This has resulted in some large, relatively level areas dissected by river valleys, leading to land of an open character with relatively few sharp topographic rises. The south-western and southern fringes of Aberdeenshire are very high and formed by the Cairngorms, Lochnagar and the Mounth, where extensive alpine habitat grades down into large moorlands and peatlands. There are some large native pinewoods, mainly in Deeside as well as a high cover of plantation forestry, dominated by Scots Pine. Central and south-eastern Aberdeenshire is a mosaic of improved agricultural land, forestry, woodland and moorland. The Aberdeenshire coast is very varied, composed mainly of hard rock cliffs, but with some extensive sand dune complexes and coastal heath. The rivers North Esk, Dee, Don, Ythan and Deveron are the main watercourses, but there are relatively few major bodies of standing water. Where the Dee and Don meet the North Sea lies the City of Aberdeen, which has much countryside within its boundary and scattered remnants of semi-natural habitat within the built-up area.

The range of habitats in North-East Scotland, together with its northerly location and affinities with the Atlantic, Boreal and Alpine zones of Europe, leads to a very rich and varied flora and fauna. 'Semi-natural' vegetation such as moorland, mountain, peat bogs and broad-leaved woodland cover around one-third of the land surface and there is an extensive and wild coastline with a large sea area of varying characteristics. Thus, in addition to birds, there are many species worth searching for and a trip to any of the bird localities in this guide is likely to reveal much interesting wildlife. Below is only a brief introduction to the richness of the area.

Wild flowers, mosses, lichens and fungi

Twinflower *I. Francis*

Of most interest to botanists are species with a northern affinity and those living in high mountain habitats, especially in wet flushes and near snow patches. Some northern plants are widespread over the area, such as the largely woodland flower, the Chickweed Wintergreen (which was described as new to science from a specimen near Aberdeen in 1620), or the moorland Bearberry, but others are more special and often sought out, such as the Twinflower, Alpine Blue Sow-thistle or Yellow Marsh Saxifrage. There are some notable botanical areas in the eastern Cairngorms, such as around Glen Clunie and Glen Callater/Corrie Kander near Braemar, where base-rich rocks influence the high-altitude flora. Our native pine woodlands are another special feature, with the best examples at Glen Tanar, Ballochbuie and Mar Lodge. These may contain Creeping Lady's Tresses, Twinflower and wintergreens (including the scarce Intermediate Wintergreen), with Juniper scrub widespread both within them and on many moorlands. Birch woods are characteristic of the north-east too and Morrone Birkwood, on rich rocks west of Braemar, has many interesting species of plants and fungi, similar to Scandinavian woodlands. The river bank grasslands along the Dee, mown to allow fly-fishing, are also worth exploring, often holding Spignel, Globeflower or Maiden Pink.

Oysterplant *I. Francis*

Plants with more southern affinities such as Clustered Bellflower and the scarce Nottingham Catchfly are found on the coast around St. Cyrus, which is another rich botanical locality. Also along the Aberdeenshire coast there is around 70 km^2 of sand dune habitat, comprising some of the largest and best examples in the country. Despite an important part being destroyed by a golf course in 2010, a visit to dune slacks along the Foveran to Forvie Sands coast is well worthwhile, as is also one to the dune slacks near Loch of Strathbeg and Rattray Head. Scattered on some other coastal strandlines (such as near Logie Head by Cullen) is the attractive Oysterplant, a species of generally northern distribution.

One notable feature of the north-east is the serpentine-rich rock which outcrops at the Green Hill of Strathdon, the Coyles of Muick near Ballater and Hill of Towanreef near Rhynie. These are some of the largest in the UK and hold a unique flora influenced by rocks rich in calcium, iron and magnesium, with metal tolerant species such as Spring Sandwort, Mossy Saxifrage and Thrift widespread. There are also areas of montane willow scrub at high altitudes in the area, holding Downy, Woolly and Whortle Willows. In several areas, for example Glen Muick, there are Dwarf Birch woodlands, another northern species.

Some other flowering plants for which North-East Scotland is notable (or which are northern species that can be found here) include Coralroot Orchid, Small Cow-wheat, Alpine Lady's Mantle, Alpine Foxtail, Northern Rock-cress, Alpine Milk-vetch, Alpine Mouse-ear, Mountain Avens, Trailing Azalea, Curved Wood-rush, Spignel, Alpine Meadow-grass and Moss Campion.

The native pine woodlands, peat bogs and montane flushes and ledges provide excellent habitat for many uncommon and northern species of moss (such as the Green Shield Moss), abundant lichens (often luxuriant on trees, indicating good air quality) and a very rich community of fungi. The mountains are very important in a UK context for arctic-alpine fungi, and the semi-natural pinewoods at Mar Lodge and Glen Tanar are very rich in pine-associated species, many of which are known only from Scotland within the UK – for example, the Devil's Tooth.

Devil's Tooth Fungus *L. Holden*

Other habitats, including dune systems, semi-improved grasslands and riverine woodland, can also contain interesting fungal communities. The Muir of Dinnet, Craig Leek, Glen Clunie and Glas Maol are also important sites for fungi. The area around Creag Clunie, The Lion's Face and Craig Leek near Braemar is of great significance for lichens, holding, for example, the rare Elm Gyalecta lichen, and Beinn a' Bhuird to Ben Avon are also important sites, along with Mar Lodge. Montane flushes and ledges also hold a range of 'red-listed' moss species such as Alpine Sulphur Tresses, and the scarce liverwort, Stabler's Rustwort, grows in flushes in the Cairngorms area.

Invertebrates – butterflies, moths and dragonflies

Pearl-bordered Fritillary *N. Littlewood*

A wide range of butterflies and moths is present in the area, with some notable species. Woodlands and the edges of upland heaths in Deeside especially hold the decreasing Pearl-bordered Fritillary, and wetter unimproved pastures and some coastal grasslands hold Small Pearl-bordered Fritillary. Scotch Argus is characteristic of some similar habitats in western parts. Moorlands hold the Large Heath and these may still survive on a few lowland raised bogs. On the coast, Graylings can be abundant and often share these sites with the more widespread Dark Green Fritillary. Small Blues are common at a few sites along and close to the north coast, and Northern Brown Argus can be found on the coast between Aberdeen and Stonehaven as well as in the eastern Cairngorms. Many of the species in the north-east can be seen by visiting the Dinnet area in Deeside and the coast between Muchalls and Stonehaven, such as the Skatie Shore.

Kentish Glory
R.Leverton

A range of moth species can be found that are specialities of northern areas. Young Birch woodlands on Deeside can hold Kentish Glory whilst Rannoch Sprawler and Cousin German are found in older woods. Dark-bordered Beauty is found in two Aspen sites – this species is present in just four other locations in Britain. Bearberry moorland holds Netted Mountain Moth and the now very rare Small Dark Yellow Underwing. On the mountains, specialities include Northern Dart, Scotch Burnet and Black Mountain Moth.

Of the 12 species of dragonflies and damselflies in the area, the Northern Damselfly is the most noteworthy, with a cluster of sites for this northern species around the Muir of Dinnet. The White-faced Darter has also been recorded at this site in recent years. The ponds at Castle Fraser near Kemnay are also good for dragonflies, including the Northern and Azure Damselflies.

Northern Damselfly *I. Francis*

Other land and freshwater invertebrates

A vast range of other invertebrates is found in the area. The Freshwater Pearl Mussel is present in several places in the North-east. It is classified as Endangered globally (and Critically Endangered in Europe). Populations in Aberdeenshire's rivers are declining, with only one river where breeding is still thought to occur.

Fresh water pearl mussels *D. Shields Alba Ecology*

Scottish Wood Ant mound *I. Francis*

Elsewhere, either no juveniles have been produced for decades or the mussels have died out.

Scottish Wood Ants are widespread in woodlands in upper Deeside and the rare Narrow-headed Wood Ant is present in pinewoods on the Mar Lodge Estate. Other examples of invertebrate richness include the rare snail *Vertigo alpestris,* found at Craig Leek near Braemar, and *Vertigo angustior*, present just north of Stonehaven. Several montane species with affinities to the arctic are found on the Cairngorms, including weevils and sawflies. More conspicuously, the red-listed Five-spot Ladybird has recently been found on unstable shingle along the River Dee.

Freshwater fish, reptiles and amphibians

Atlantic Salmon *J. Urquhart RDT*

The Dee, Don, North Esk and Ythan are renowned as important rivers for Atlantic Salmon or Sea Trout, and Salmon can be seen ascending waterfalls in several places at certain times of year, notably the Bridge of Feugh near Banchory. Associated with Salmon, the Dee, Don and North Esk also hold River, Sea and Brook Lampreys (the latter is the commonest) and Eels are also present in several rivers. Brown Trout are widespread in rivers and lochs, but one of the rarest fish is the Arctic Charr – an ice-age relic, found in a very few upland lochs.

The amphibian and reptile fauna is limited due to the area's northerly location; species likely to be encountered are Common Frog, Common Toad (both widespread), Palmate Newt, Common Lizard (widespread), Adder (present locally in good numbers especially around Glen Girnock and Ballater) and Slow-worm.

Adder *I. Francis*

Land mammals

Around 45 species of land mammals are found in North-East Scotland. Some are elusive and rarely seen; others are spreading in or escaped from captivity (such as Wild Boar which has been recorded recently). European Beavers are not yet here but are present just to the south in Angus. One of our most distinctive mammals is the Red Squirrel, which is common and whose population here forms the south-eastern edge of its large Scottish Highlands range. Grey Squirrels, present in the Aberdeen area, are being culled to prevent them spreading into this stronghold.

Mountain Hare *C. Komlosi*

Another species, currently making a comeback after intense efforts to control the predatory American Mink, is the Water Vole – many of which in the area are almost black in colour. Some of the strongholds for this species are high altitude burns in the mountains. By contrast, the Otter is widespread and regularly seen at lochs such as Davan and Strathbeg, though rarely on the coast. Mountain Hares are common on mountains and upland deer estates especially around Braemar, but increasingly less common on grouse moorlands, where they are culled.

Red Deer Stags Mar Lodge *I. Francis*

Two species of deer are very common in the area. Roe Deer are found everywhere from mountain to coast, and large numbers of Red Deer are present in upper Deeside and Donside. It is easily possible to see over 1,000 Red Deer on a drive over Glen Shee to Braemar. In terms of predators, the Pine Marten has recovered much of its former range and is now widespread in North-east Scotland. By contrast, the Scottish Wildcat is now very rare and threatened. However, several of its remaining strongholds are within or close to the area, including the Angus Glens to the south, the Strathbogie area south of Huntly and Strathavon to the north-west. Finally, six species of bat have been recorded recently, none nationally rare, with the most widespread species being Common Pipistrelle, Brown Long-eared and Daubenton's.

Marine life

Seabirds are clearly an extremely important feature of North-East Scotland's marine environment, but many other species are found beneath the high tide mark – though specialist equipment is often needed to search for them! There are though some very good areas of intertidal rocky habitat. The shore lines between Rosehearty and Fraserburgh and between Inverbervie and Gourdon are very extensive and their rock pools are well worth searching. On a smaller scale, rocky shores and cliffs form much of the coast, and the extensive beaches also provide strandlines with interesting finds washed up. Marine fish are rarely observed, but the Sand Goby is common in the Ythan Estuary.

Watches from shore can reveal a range of dolphins and whales, and boat trips are possible from several harbours offering close encounters (which might also include Basking Shark, now becoming more common off the coast). Harbour Porpoises and Bottlenose Dolphins are the most frequently seen species and these are widespread offshore; in particular, the mouth of Aberdeen Harbour often produces excellent views of Bottlenose Dolphins. Other species seen regularly (mostly in summer) include White-beaked Dolphin and Minke Whale. Humpback Whale is now recorded most years and formerly rarer species are becoming increasingly frequent including Killer and Sperm Whales. The most common marine mammals, though, are both Grey and Common Seals, with good views possible in most areas around the coast and in particular at the mouth of the Ythan Estuary where several hundred now haul out in summer. Donmouth can also be good for close views, along with the fish quay area of Peterhead Harbour where Grey Seals loiter for scraps.

Bottlenose Dolphin *H. Scott*

Some key bird species: how, where and when

Pink-footed Goose

Spectacular concentrations of these geese are found in the area, throughout the winter from mid-September to early May, but especially in October and November (and again in April), when much of the Iceland/Greenland flyway population passes through. The best places to watch dawn and dusk flights are the Loch of Strathbeg (up to 60,000 birds), the Ythan Estuary and Meikle Loch (20,000), Loch of Skene (15-20,000) and in the south of the area where tens of thousands fly towards the Montrose Basin.

King Eider

The large concentrations of Common Eiders in our area often attract King Eider. This beautiful duck can be looked for on the Ythan Estuary (downstream of the Waterside Bridge, check around the Inch Road, and towards the river mouth) and at Blackdog where large post-breeding concentrations of moulting drake Common Eiders can hold King Eider. The species can be found throughout the year anywhere along the coast.

King Eider *N. Littlewood*

These birds are long lived, and regular birds can turn up year after year (including "Elvis" which was seen from the late 1980s until 2000). However, there are less than annual records from 2000.

Common, Velvet and Surf Scoters

The coast from the Donmouth at Aberdeen north to the Ythan holds large numbers of scoters and eiders, peaking in late summer but present all year. Around 3,000 Common Scoters can be seen, with tens (sometimes low hundreds) of Velvet Scoters and annually a very small number of Surf Scoters. Rarer species of scoter have also been found in the flocks. The best viewpoints are from Blackdog and Murcar, and June to August is a good time to look for these birds.

Surf Scoter *N. Littlewood*

Ptarmigan

Most hills over 900m hold this species in varying densities, and a high-level walk should ensure an encounter, especially around steeper areas with rocky outcrops. The most accessible areas are around the Cairnwell at the Glen Shee ski area and Morven (mid-Deeside). Highest densities are found along the Mounth hills, especially Lochnagar. Flocks of tens of birds can be found in the autumn in some places.

Black Grouse

Aberdeenshire holds around 700-800 lekking Black Grouse – a significant proportion of the national population. Most are in Upper Deeside. From March to May, they can be seen or heard fairly easily in the Glen Muick and Mar Lodge areas, along with the Forest of Birse and numerous other areas. Some leks are in secluded places, and all are prone to disturbance, so please do not approach them. During the rest of the year a walk along tracks near most forests in upper Deeside or upper Donside gives a chance of an encounter.

Capercaillie *M. Sullivan*

Capercaillie

Though long associated with Deeside, this bird is now very rare in the area, with probably fewer than 100 remaining. There are no sites where they can be viewed without causing disturbance – they are specially protected by law. However, walks along tracks in any of the large pinewoods or plantations may provide a chance, especially in the autumn or winter.

White-billed Diver

Divers of the three most familiar species (Red-throated, Great Northern and the rarer Black-throated) can be seen off any coastal area, with large numbers (hundreds) of Red-throated off the east coast in spring. Tens of Great Northern Divers can be seen in late winter off Rattray Head and Inverallochy. More recently, small numbers of White-billed Divers (up to 20 birds) have been present regularly each spring off the north coast, and can be most reliably looked for (with a telescope) from the Portsoy area. Boat trips can be organised from Macduff or Buckie in April - early May which can provide close-up views of these birds.

White-billed Diver *M. Sullivan*

Gannet

Gannet *M. Sullivan*

Widespread around the whole coast, a trip to the Troup Head RSPB reserve near Pennan is certainly worthwhile for excellent close-up views of the breeding colony (the only one on the mainland Scottish coast). Over 2,000 pairs nest here, and birds can be seen on the cliffs from around March to the end of September.

Red Kite

A re-introduction programme was begun by the RSPB in 2007. Following the release over three years of 101 young birds near Peterculter, by 2014 there were 25 breeding pairs. Together with non-breeders, this means there are perhaps 150-200 kites around the Aberdeen area, and they can be seen in many places. Good areas to look are in the Garlogie, Drumoak and Dunecht areas, with increasing numbers in the south towards Edzell.

Red Kite *J. Young*

Golden and White-tailed Eagles

Golden Eagles are rare birds in the area, with only around 15 breeding pairs. Upper Deeside and the Cairngorms provide the best opportunity to see the birds. Scan the sky around Braemar and over any of the tributary glens of the Dee as far east as Aboyne. White-tailed Eagles from the re-introduction in Fife have been seen increasingly regularly in Deeside and Donside, so all eagles should be checked carefully! In winter White-tailed Eagles might be found at or near the coast, especially where concentrations of geese occur.

White-tailed Eagle *R. Humphreys*

Osprey

Around 20 pairs of Ospreys nest in Aberdeenshire. They are present from early April to late September. As breeding birds they are scattered, but feeding birds can be seen along any major river, particularly the lower Don and Ythan, and the Ythan Estuary can hold several feeding birds at once, particularly in August. At the Lochter Activity Centre near Oldmeldrum (www.Lochter.co.uk), a pair nests on an artificial platform and can be watched on a CCTV monitor from the comfort of the restaurant. Other fisheries can also be productive, such as Auchnagatt, Midmar, Raemoir and Strachan.

Osprey chicks *E. Weston*

Common Crane

Common Crane and chick *H. Maggs*

Common Cranes have become more frequent and more widespread in the area over recent years. Since 2012, following the first nesting in Scotland of modern times, a very small and vulnerable breeding population is now present. For the future success of this species, it is critical that they are not visited, as they are very susceptible to disturbance. Cranes are, however, frequently seen as migrants, especially in late spring, in several coastal areas such as the Loch of Strathbeg and near the Ythan Estuary, and these offer the best and most responsible chance of seeing them.

Dotterel

In summer up to 200 male Dotterel may be present on the high tops of Aberdeenshire and the Cairngorms. Most of the high mountains provide an opportunity to see or hear them, though there are no reliable lower altitude sites – all require a serious hill walk! They are specially protected by law, so ensure you do not disturb them if you find them.

Seabirds

As well as Gannet, the Aberdeenshire coast holds some very large, internationally important colonies of other seabirds – they are truly some of our most impressive natural sights. The best places to see cliff-nesting seabirds are the Fowlsheugh RSPB reserve south of Stonehaven, the Bullers of Buchan north of Cruden Bay, and the stretch of coast from Pennan Head westwards past Troup Head to Gardenstown. Puffins can be seen at all these colonies (probably best at Bullers of Buchan and just north of Fowlsheugh around Dunnottar Castle), and can also be seen off Muchalls, just north of Stonehaven. Black Guillemots are scarce in the area and best seen along the north coast, where they breed in small numbers. One or two pairs can also be seen at Newtonhill / Muchalls. The best locality to see breeding terns is the Ythan Estuary and Sands of Forvie NNR, which holds the largest Sandwich Tern colony in Scotland (high hundreds of pairs) along with good numbers of Common and Arctic Terns with a few tens of Little Terns. There are also Common and Arctic Tern colonies at the Loch of Strathbeg reserve, and they breed at other scattered localities; Common Terns may nest inland along rivers and in some industrial estates. Terns can be seen anywhere along the coast from April to September.

Puffin *M. Sullivan*

Waxwing

Waxwing *M. Sullivan*

Although Waxwings can be seen during invasion years almost anywhere in the UK, Aberdeen is one of the most consistent places from winter to winter, and nowadays birds turn up virtually every year. There can be some impressive gatherings of hundreds of birds in Aberdeen's street trees and cemeteries; anywhere with berry-bearing trees in winter is worth investigating, such as Kincorth, Hilton and Bridge of Don. A regular haunt is opposite the car sale rooms on the Lang Stracht, off the A90 in the west of the city. Inverurie, Westhill, Banchory and Aboyne, along with some other rural towns, also regularly hold birds.

Crossbills

Three species of crossbill breed in Aberdeenshire - Common, Parrot and Scottish. Common Crossbills are widespread across the area in almost any conifer plantation. Parrot Crossbills are found in very small numbers in the old pinewoods and plantations of Upper Deeside. Scottish Crossbills (the UK's only endemic bird species) are found in a range of plantation types and native pine forests, mainly in the west of the area. All three species could be found in the same woodlands. It is important to stress that the numbers of all three species can vary greatly from year to year depending on the abundance of different types of conifer cones. It is definitely worth stating that identification can be extremely difficult. The extremes of Common Crossbill and Parrot Crossbill can be more straightforward, but there are many intermediates, with calls overlapping too. Careful observations are needed!

Left to right: Common, Scottish and Parrot Crossbills. These photographs in the hand of the three species taken in Deeside indicate the differences in head and bill shape and structure which need to be considered carefully when attempting field identification. Viewing the birds well can be difficult in many situations and they are very challenging. Photographs: Rab Rae. For further details see: Rae, R. 2010. Crossbills – some clues for their identification in the field. Scottish Birds 30: 178-185.

Snow Bunting

In winter, Snow Buntings are frequently seen around the coast (try the Ythan dunes) and often in small flocks in stubble fields on farmland anywhere. They also stay around the uplands, particularly at the two main ski centres at the Lecht and Glen Shee – check the car park edges! A few tens of birds breed in the mountains, on the highest rocky tops. Visiting the Cairngorm plateau or Lochnagar in summer could well yield a sighting of flying or singing birds. They are specially protected as breeding birds and care should be taken not to disturb them – though sometimes they can be very tame!

Snow Bunting *M. Sullivan*

Corn Bunting

Corn Bunting
M. Sullivan

Increasingly scarce across much of the UK, North-East Scotland still holds good numbers of this bird in certain areas, in part due to management schemes initiated by RSPB Scotland and sustained by agricultural support schemes. The best areas to search lie on farmland close to the coast from Rattray Head westwards to Banff, and especially south of Rosehearty and Fraserburgh, where some of the highest breeding densities in the UK are found, with some large winter flocks at times.

Migration hotspots and sea-watching sites

The coast of North-East Scotland is well-known as a great place to find migrant birds. During April to June and from late July to November there is nearly always something moving. At times, there can be big movements of seabirds, or 'falls' of small bird migrants, in certain weather conditions. Waders move in spring and autumn too, and there are some favoured places for all these, most of which are indentified in the site accounts. The list below covers some of the main sites, from north to south, all of which are worth checking.

Rosehearty to Fraserburgh coast: waders, ducks, passing geese and seabirds.

Kinnaird Head, Fraserburgh: seabirds present almost all year, with some large, close movements at times.

Loch of Strathbeg RSPB Reserve: this extensive wetland site can attract large numbers of migrants of all kinds, with seabirds offshore.

Rattray Head: a fine place to search for migrant birds in the bushes and low vegetation, waders on the pools and seabirds offshore.

Peterhead Harbour: seabird movements can be seen well here.

Cruden Bay woodlands: worth searching for migrant passerines in autumn.

Meikle Loch RSPB reserve: if water levels are low, it can be attractive to migrant waders. There are also other small, seasonal pools in the nearby Slains area which can attract migrant waders.

Collieston: the trees and shrubs along the gully towards the village are a renowned place to look for migrant birds, and offshore can be good for seabirds.

Ythan Estuary: very good for migrants of all kinds for much of the year, with waders, ducks and geese on the estuary. The Foveran bushes on the south side of the estuary mouth are often good for holding rarer passerine species.

Balmedie Country Park: the bushes round the car parks are worth searching for migrant birds in autumn.

Blackdog: coastal bushes and foreshore should be checked, and many sea ducks and seabirds can be seen offshore, including visible migration at times.

Girdle Ness, Aberdeen: One of the best migration watch points for seabirds and always produces many passerine migrants, including rarities. There are many suitable bushes and cover to search.

Rigifa Pool, Cove: worth checking for migrant waders.

St. Cyrus: waders, geese and migrant songbirds can all be seen here.

Visible migration

At certain times, especially in autumn, weather conditions can lead to large and continuous movements of a range of migrating birds throughout the day, known as 'visible migration'. In North-East Scotland this spectacle is best seen along the coast, at watch points such as Blackdog. The species involved are mostly British populations of open country birds such as swallows and martins, pipits, wagtails and finches heading for more southerly winter quarters. A notable exception is the onward passage of Icelandic Pink-footed Geese heading south from staging posts at Strathbeg and the Ythan which can be spectacular. September and October are the best months, and most passage occurs in the first few hours after dawn on days with a light to moderate south-westerly to westerly cross-wind which pushes birds migrating over the land onto the coast, which they then follow southwards. The best days are when these conditions follow several days of inclement weather, often in the clearing conditions immediately following the passage of a cold front. The best sites are probably those further south as this increases the potential catchment area for birds coming from the north. Blackdog is the only site that has been consistently watched to date, but the north side of Donmouth should also be good (5,000 Skylarks were estimated passing south here on 24th December 1995), and the coast between Johnshaven and St. Cyrus has good geography for concentrating visible migrants and would repay visits.

Highlights from watches at Blackdog (Nick Littlewood) during 2010-2012 include 13,762 Pink-footed Geese on 6th October 2011, a Rough-legged Buzzard on 7th November 2009, a Pallid Harrier first seen on the Ythan Estuary which passed over on 1st October 2011, 2,565 Meadow Pipits on 14th September 2010, 194 Pied Wagtails on 26th September 2011, 90 Waxwings on 28th October 2010, 630 Linnets on 6th October 2011 and Lapland Buntings on two dates in 2010.

For seabirds, the stronger the winds the better and east to north-easterlies help push birds onto the coast. Many seabirds tend to head north and the NNE-SSW trending coast suggests that the best sites are likely to be those northwards along the coast, with more birds closer in moving from Girdle Ness to Boddam/Peterhead and Kinnaird Head, Fraserburgh.

Recording birds and wildlife in North-East Scotland

When visiting any of the sites in this guide, you will see interesting and noteworthy things! Make sure you pass on your records to the right place so they can help build up a picture of our local birds and other wildlife, and contribute to improving our knowledge for conservation and for science.

For **birds**: please send your records to the North-East Scotland Bird Recorder, whose details can always be found on the recording webpage of the Scottish Ornithologists' Club - www.the-soc.org.uk/bird-recording/local-recorders-network/north-east-scotland-recording-area.

If you use BirdTrack, (www.bto.org/volunteer-surveys/birdtrack/about), records will also be passed to the local recorder.

For **all other wildlife**: please send your records to the North-East Scotland Biological Records Centre (www.nesbrec.org.uk).

Further Information

Buckland, S.T., Bell, M.V. & Picozzi, N. (eds). 1990. *The Birds of North-East Scotland*. North-East Scotland Bird Club, Aberdeen.

Francis, I. & Cook, M. (eds) 2011. *The Breeding Birds of North-East Scotland*. Scottish Ornithologists' Club, Aberdeen.

Jenkins, D. (ed.) 2013. *Birds in mid-Deeside 1970-2012*. Swallowtail Print. Norwich.

Marren, P. 1982 *A Natural History of Aberdeen* R. Callander, Finzean (out of print).

North-East Scotland Bird Reports (produced annually). North-East Scotland Bird Club.

Phillips, I.M. 1997. *Rare and Scarce Birds in North East Scotland*. Privately Published.

Shaw, P. & Thompson, D.B.A. (eds.) 2006. *The Nature of the Cairngorms: diversity in a changing environment*. The Stationery Office, Edinburgh.

Watson, A. and Francis, I. 2012. *Birds in north-east Scotland then and now*. Paragon Publishing, Northants.

Welch, D. 1993. *Flora of North Aberdeenshire. Botanical vice-county 93*. Privately published, D. Welch, Banchory.

Web Resources

Bird news - local grapevine information
www.groups.yahoo.com/neo/groups/ABZ-Rare-Birds/info

North-East Scotland Biological Records Centre (NESBReC)
www.nesbrec.org.uk

North-East Scotland Local Biodiversity Action Plan
www.nesbiodiversity.org.uk

You can also find out about local birds from RSPB Scotland's Aberdeen Office
www.rspb.org.uk/contactus/offices/scotland/eastscotland.aspx

Local Contacts

Aberdeen and District RSPB Local Group:	www.rspb.org.uk/groups/aberdeen	
RSPB East Scotland Regional Office:	esro@rspb.org.uk	01224 624824
SSPCA (for any injured birds):		03000 999 999
SOC:	www.the-soc.org.uk/whats-on/local-branches-2/grampian	
Wildlife Crime (Police):		0845 6005700

1. IN AND AROUND ABERDEEN

Girdle Ness from Aberdeen Harbour *F. Sullivan*

The City of Aberdeen contains many excellent bird-watching sites, with both breeding and migrant birds giving year-round interest. The city centre itself, with its parks, gardens and tree-lined streets hold interest. Peregrines breed in the centre - check around the old Marischal College building (now the Council Offices). Skeins of Pink-footed Geese pass overhead in autumn to spring, and birds such as Dipper and Grey Wagtail can be seen in winter. Winter also brings mass arrivals of thrushes, and, in many winters, Waxwings, which feast on the abundant rowan berries in various cemeteries and in the surrounding streets. **Johnston Gardens**, **Allenvale**, **Springbank** and **King St. Cemeteries** are all worth a visit.

Peregrine chick
J. Weston

The City lies between two rivers, the Dee to the south, and the Don to the north, and contains many parks and river walks where a wide variety of birds can be seen. In addition are the river mouth of the Don, and the built-up harbour at the mouth of the Dee. The various rocky headlands and sand dunes along the coast to the south and north respectively provide both nesting sites for a range of species, but more importantly act as magnets for spring and autumn migrants, as well as acting as sea-watching sites of great potential. Some of the most productive of these sites are described below.

Girdle Ness (NJ 965 055)

Location & access: Girdle Ness is the headland immediately to the south of Aberdeen Harbour. Greyhope Road runs round the perimeter offering various parking areas from which to explore. The car parks at Torry Battery, Greyhope and Nigg Bays also allow some birding from the car to be undertaken.

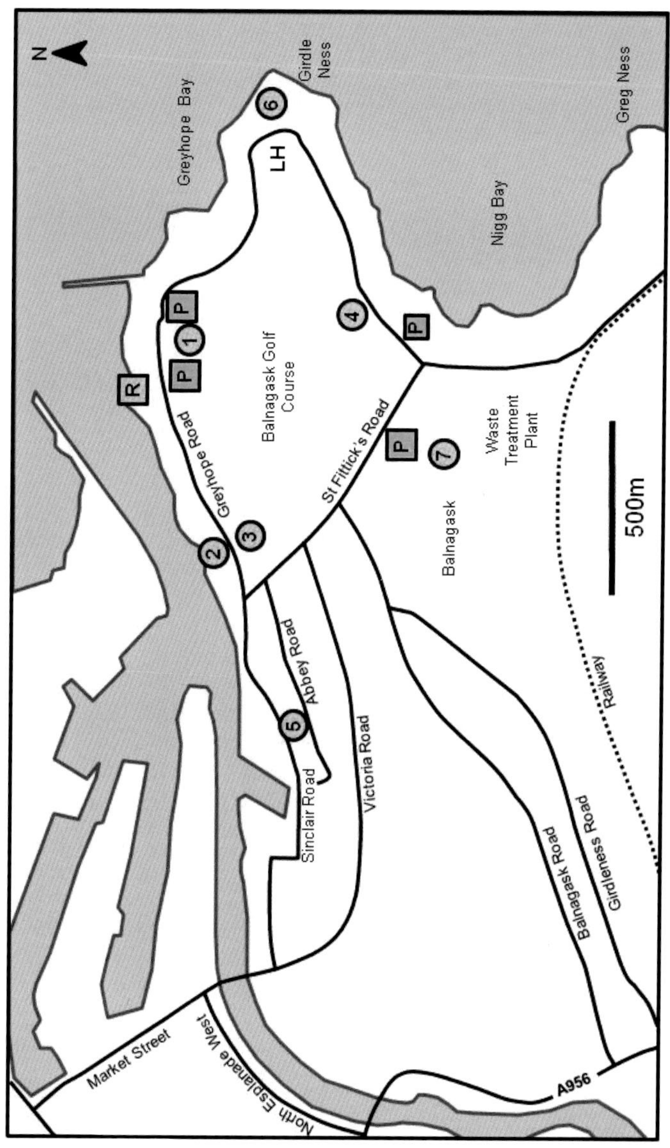

Habitat and potential wildlife: Most of the area is a golf course with a lighthouse on the headland, a series of allotments on the harbour side, and the rocky Greyhope and Nigg Bays. There is always something of interest to be seen with all year birding enhanced by the presence of Grey Seals, and in particular the regular occurrence of Bottlenose Dolphins in the harbour mouth. Porpoises are also occasionally seen, with other cetacean species also noted offshore by keen observers. During spring and autumn the best conditions are a gentle southeast breeze with mist or drizzle, and during these times almost anything can turn up. The best areas for migrants at Girdle Ness are the gorse and shrubs around Torry Battery (the ruined fort on the hilltop (**1**)), and the Sycamore trees below the allotments near the harbour mouth, as well as the allotments themselves (**2+3**). To the south, there is another area of gorse and scrub, known as the 'South Bank' situated on the golf course by the northern edge of Nigg Bay (**4**). In the right conditions almost any patch of cover can hold birds such as Red-backed Shrike, Bluethroat and Wryneck fairly regularly. Rarities such as Icterine Warbler, Red-breasted Flycatcher, Radde's Warbler, Isabelline Wheatear, Lesser Grey and Woodchat Shrikes have occurred.

Bluethroat *M. Sullivan*

Slightly inland, Abbey Road (**5**) has berry-bearing trees and wasteland that are very attractive to Waxwings, thrushes, warblers and finches during autumn.

The foghorn by the lighthouse is an established sea-watching point (**6**). The commoner skuas and shearwaters are regular during late summer - early autumn, and there is always the chance of something rarer; Cory's Shearwater has been seen. A large moult flock of Eiders builds up from late June, and can hold 800 or more birds around the foghorn and the adjacent Nigg Bay.

The winter months usually produce a few records of Glaucous and Iceland Gulls, often in the harbour.

Purple Sandpipers *M. Sullivan*

Girdle Ness is also a local stronghold for Purple Sandpiper, with large numbers (>150) roosting either on the middle breakwater on the south side of the harbour (**R**), or among the rocks and shingle of Greyhope Bay. With them are Turnstones, Redshanks, Oystercatchers and Ringed Plovers, with small numbers of other waders.

Auks are often seen, Guillemot being most common, but Razorbill, Black Guillemot and Puffin can also be found. Little Auks are recorded in bad weather passing the headland in winter, and Brunnich's Guillemot has been recorded once off the harbour.

In summer, Common, Arctic and Sandwich Terns are present, feeding in the harbour mouth. When mackerel are running, large numbers of Gannets can be watched plunge diving just offshore. Breeding Linnets, Goldfinches, Skylarks and both Meadow and Rock Pipits can all be found around the headland.

Immediately inland from Nigg Bay a low damp area has been re-landscaped with the creation of several ponds, and the re-profiling of the East Tullos Burn (**7**). Historically this was a good wader site, with spring and autumn passage of Ruff, Little Stint and other species. It is hoped that the 2014 redevelopment will allow the site to regain its interest. It is also good for Common Darter dragonflies. Scrub and woodland along the railway line and the waste treatment plant can also be productive for migrants. Records in 2014 have included Yellow-browed and Blyth's Reed Warbler, Citrine Wagtail and Tundra Bean Goose.

Inchgarth Reservoir (NJ 902 027)

Location & access: Located 8km west of the city centre this site allows the opportunity to see some of the characteristic birds of the lower River Dee and its surrounding woodlands. From the A90 Bridge of Dee roundabout, take the minor (Garthdee) road westwards past Asda and B&Q. After about 3km, look for the entrance to the reservoir. This is located on the left after the turn-off signposted to Cults. Park carefully and do not block the access gates.

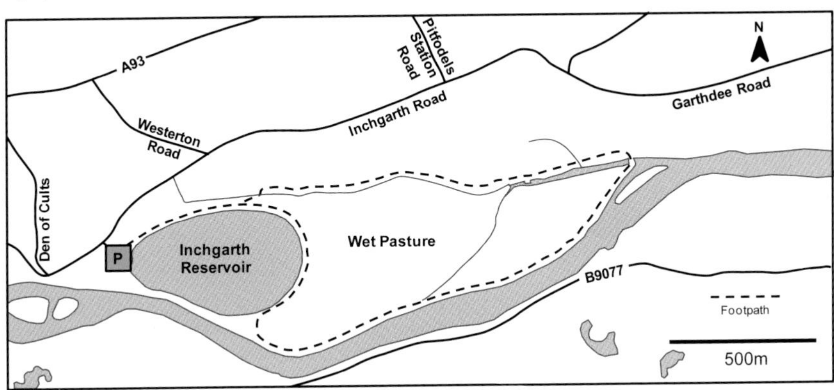

Enter through the pedestrian gate and scope the reservoir from the boundary fence. Follow the road around the reservoir. Just before the pumping station a path heads southwards towards the River Dee. Continue along the river bank downstream. After a wooden boardwalk turn left and uphill, before heading west through mixed woodland back to the reservoir and the start of the walk. Note that in times of flood this walk is not accessible.

Habitat and potential wildlife: A concrete reservoir on the bank of the River Dee, it has mixed woodland and wet pasture bounding the northern and eastern sides respectively. The site has year-round interest, with typical riverine and woodland birds.

Inchgarth Reservoir *I. Francis*

From September onwards increasing numbers of duck occur; over 100 Wigeon, 50-100 Goldeneye and up to 150 Goosanders have been noted. Smaller numbers of Tufted Duck, Mallard, Teal and Red-breasted Merganser are seen regularly.

Jack Snipe *I. Auchterlonie*

Red and Black-throated Divers, Little, Slavonian, Great Crested and Red-necked Grebes have also been recorded. There are often large numbers of gulls seen here with occasional white-winged gulls among them. Jack Snipe are regular in the wet pasture immediately east of the reservoir (accessed through a gate). The overgrown nature of this area makes working it difficult, but birds can be found from October through to spring and Water Rail are noted in winter. In hard weather Kingfishers and Water Rails can be found in the ditches within the woodland. The River Dee around here is probably the best place to look for Kingfishers in Aberdeen.

During spring and autumn, Ospreys pass through here, but they rarely stop and waders such as Green Sandpiper and Greenshank are seen in small numbers. Oystercatchers gather here in good numbers in mid-February before moving inland to breed.

Whitethroat *G. Holm*

In summer, the woodland holds breeding Chiffchaff, Blackcap, Garden and Willow Warblers, with reeling Grasshopper Warbler on the wet pasture. On the river Kingfisher, Dipper, Common Sandpiper and Grey Wagtail can be seen, whilst the gorse holds Whitethroat and Sedge Warblers in good numbers.

Cove Bay Area

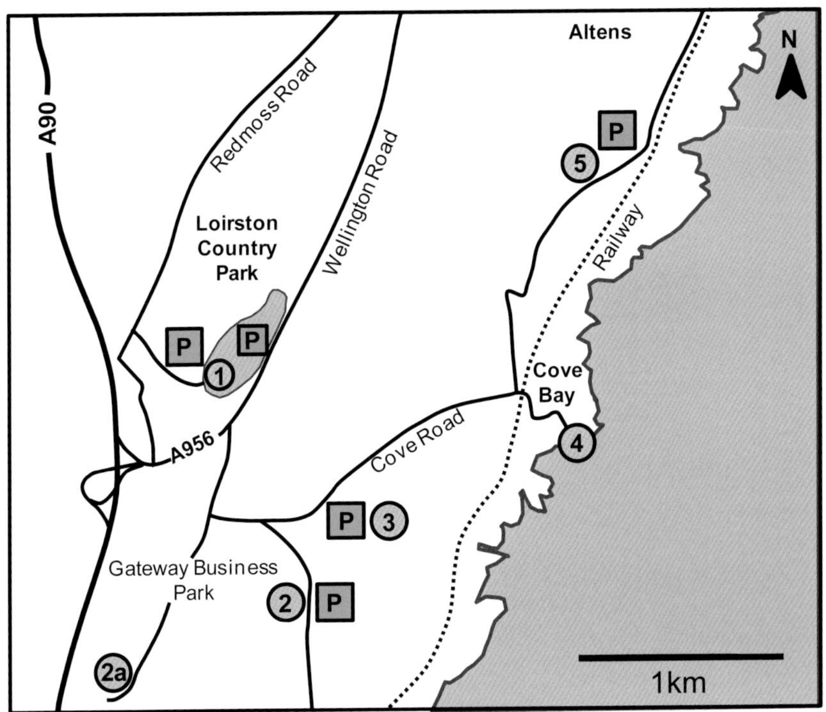

On the southern outskirts of Aberdeen, despite significant housing development in the past few years, a range of productive bird-watching areas is still available.

Loirston Loch (NJ 938 011)

Location & access: Situated to the south of Aberdeen, Loirston Loch (**1**) can be easily viewed from a lay-by on the northbound A956. A car park on the west side of the Loch (NJ 936 010) at Lochinch Farm, accessible from Redmoss Road, allows a walk along the northern shore and the adjacent woodland and pasture.

Habitat and potential wildlife: A small, fairly shallow freshwater loch, surrounded by willow scrub and farmland. A few pairs of Coot and Mallard nest here along with Little Grebe, with Mute Swans attempting to breed most years. The loch is very popular with anglers, which doubtless has an effect on the breeding birds.

Loirston Loch *M. Sullivan*

The adjacent scrub holds good numbers of breeding Sedge Warblers and Reed Buntings. Winter is usually the best time of the year with the scarcer diving ducks, grebes and divers occasionally putting in an appearance and the small gull roost sometimes hosts Glaucous Gull. Short-eared Owls have been recorded here in winter, and Buzzard, Sparrowhawk and Kestrel are regular. Osprey on passage regularly fish here.

Rigifa Pool (NO 941 998)

Location & access: This is an intermittently flooded field opposite Rigifa Farm (**2**). The pool can be easily viewed from the road. This temporary pool became famous in the 1980s, attracting Least Sandpiper. It was then drained, but has re-flooded in the past few years, and forms an important area for breeding Lapwing. There are however ongoing attempts to drain the pool and its extent can depend on weather conditions, so check locally that it is still present.

Rigifa Pool *M. Sullivan*

Temminck's Stint *M. Sullivan*

Habitat and potential wildlife: Being the only significant area of shallow, muddy fresh water in the vicinity, it regularly attracts small numbers of waders. Passage waders include both godwits, with more unusual waders (e.g. Temminck's Stint, Wood Sandpiper) often recorded. Even Avocet has had a prolonged stay here and Pectoral Sandpiper has occurred. Jack Snipe can be found during the winter months. Post-breeding flocks of Oystercatchers use the site. A regular wintering flock of Wigeon (100+ birds) is worth searching through for other ducks, which have included Garganey and Gadwall in the past. Large numbers of Curlews build up in the autumn, along with a roost of Pink-footed Geese. In summer, if wet conditions prevail, it continues to hold water and waders including breeding Lapwing.

Close by is **Marywell Pond** (**NO 933 995**) (**2a**), a small roadside pool holding breeding Tufted Duck and Little Grebe, which is always worth investigating. (Pectoral Sandpiper has been recorded here).

Cove Bay (NJ 954 007)

Location & access: The village of Cove Bay is situated on the southern outskirts of Aberdeen. The harbour can be reached by driving into 'old' Cove village, taking the bridge over the railway line opposite the Post Office on Loirston Road. After crossing the railway bridge, turn right, then left and follow the road down the steep hill to the sea, past the row of houses at the bottom, to the harbour.

The Community Woodland lies on the south side of the village, located off Cove Rd accessible from Rigifa Pool. If visiting from the north, turn right at the Post Office in Cove, without crossing the railway line. Park sensibly here, preferably on the verge where there is a small pull-in at a field gate, or near the entrance to Leith's yard.

Habitat and potential wildlife: The area consists of a variety of habitats, mainly suburban housing, with agricultural land to the south and north and a rocky coastline complete with a small harbour for the use of the local fishing community. Spring and autumn are without doubt the more productive times of the year.

Cove Community Woodland (**NJ 945 002**), (**3**) a small isolated wood consisting of Sycamore and Willow, surrounding a drained reservoir. As well as rarities, common migrants can also be present here in good numbers, particularly during fall conditions. Breeding birds in the area include Stonechat and Grasshopper Warbler. This is accessed through a small gate on Cove Road (NJ 943 003). The area has produced rarities such as Collared Flycatcher and Hume's Warbler and is always worth investigating in spring and autumn migration periods.

Cove Harbour (**4**) can be a good sea-watching point, especially during adverse weather when sitting in the car is a real advantage. Strong onshore winds can give good views of shearwaters and skuas with highlights being Long-tailed and Pomarine Skuas, Balearic Shearwater and Black Tern. The rocky coastline below the car park holds good numbers of Purple Sandpiper and Rock Pipits in winter. Peregrines can also be seen here. Bottlenose Dolphins pass by regularly offshore. Scotland's first Swinhoe's Petrel was caught here in August 2000 during a night time ringing session.

Burnbanks Plantation (**NJ 957 019**), (**5**) located north of Cove Bay on the Cove to Girdleness road. The plantation can be teeming with thrushes and warblers during the autumn, attracting Sparrowhawks. A car park is located just to the south of Burnbanks Village, and paths lead from here through the woodland.

Burnbanks Plantation *M. Sullivan*

Donmouth Area

The area to the north of the city centre also contains many outstanding bird-watching areas.

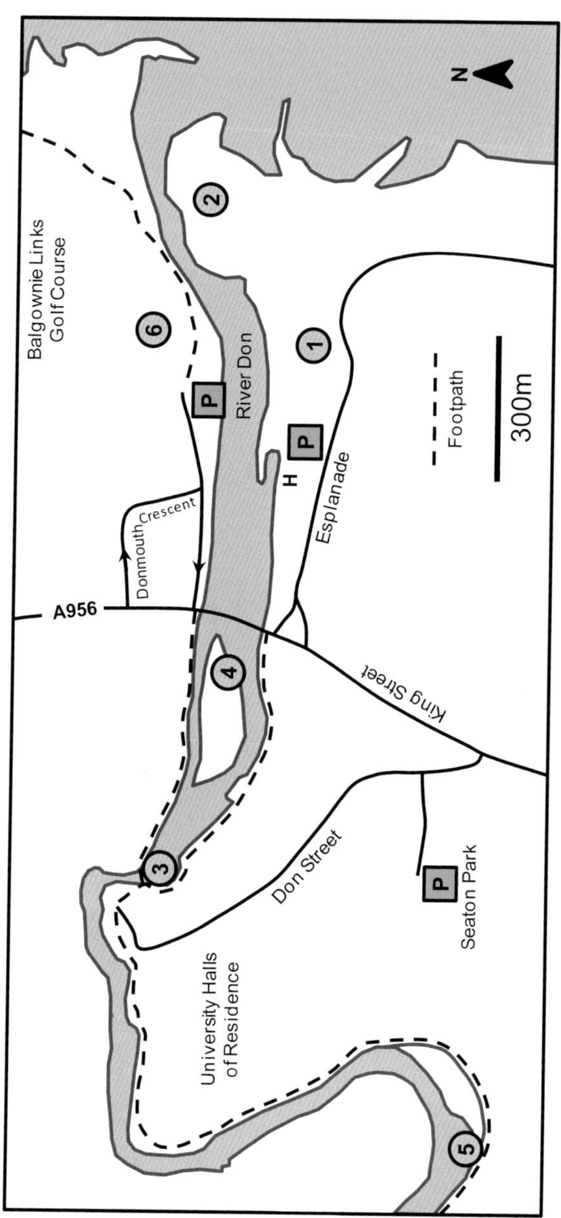

Don Estuary (NJ 953 095)

Location & access: The estuary is located at the northern end of Aberdeen Beach Esplanade where parking on the roadside allows easy access to the southern side of the estuary. A car park is also available on the north side of the estuary, on Donmouth Road allowing access to Balgownie Links (see below). The area is famous as the site of the first Lesser Sand Plover for Britain in 1991.

The estuary tends to get disturbed during the day, especially at weekends, so an early visit is usually best, especially at lower tides. Walk along the southern bank (**1**) down to the mouth of the river watching for duck, terns, gulls and waders, climb the promontory (**2**) at the mouth for an elevated sea-watching viewpoint. The hide (**H**) can give a good view over the mudflats and gull roost and adjacent bushes can hold migrants. Retracing your path westwards, and crossing the busy A92, allows a circular walk through a wooded part of the river valley to the old Brig o' Balgownie (**3**). This can be extended to Seaton Park (see next section).

Donmouth, Balgownie and Seaton Park *I Francis*

Habitat and potential wildlife: The river mouth is dominated by sand, and is constantly changing. Gorse scrub and mixed woodland occur along the south bank, and sand dunes with grasses at the mouth. During the day at low tide, waders (mainly Oystercatcher, Sanderling and Redshank) can usually be found at the mouth of the river on the beach or on the Kings Links, although some use the mudflats by the hide. At high water, if undisturbed, waders roost on a small peninsula on the south side of the estuary. Check upstream of the bridge too, where Kingfisher and Otters are seen occasionally, and the island which is a regular haul-out for Common and sometimes Grey Seals (**4**). The bushes flanking the south side of the estuary are worth checking during migration. At the mouth, on the south side, there is a small hillock with rough ground and a few bushes. These are among the best for migrants, but do not usually hold birds for long. It is always worth watching for seabirds in suitable winds (often best in northerlies), and for sea-ducks in spring. Red-throated Divers are often present in good numbers offshore.

Bar-tailed Godwit *M. Sullivan*

Seaton Park (NJ 940 092)

Location & access: Accessible from Don St (off the A956 King St south of the Bridge of Don) and parking in the car park within Seaton Park itself, or by continuing to walk up river from the River Don road bridge (see previous site).

Habitat and potential wildlife: Mostly open parkland, with mature vegetation and trees, which has the River Don running through it. Check from above the weir (**5**) for grebes, Dipper and riparian bird species. Walk downstream along the river around the north side of Hillhead Halls of Residence to see woodland birds, including singing warblers in spring. The area around the Brig o' Balgownie is good for Blackcap in spring, Kingfisher and Stock Dove.

Dipper *R. Humphreys*

This park shows that anything can turn up anywhere, as the area's only Orphean Warbler was ringed here in October 1982, and in January 2015 a 1st winter drake Harlequin was found on the River Don in the park!

1st winter Harlequin Drake *M. Sullivan*

Balgownie Links (NJ 950 096)

Location & access: From the car park on the north bank of the River Don (Donmouth Road) it is possible to walk along the seaward edge of the Royal Aberdeen golf course, viewing both the course and the sea. This area passes northwards to Blackdog, covered in the next section.

Hoopoe *T. Marshall*

Habitat and potential wildlife: Gorse bushes here tend not to be too productive, although a few small trees will attract and hold migrants in the right conditions. It is always worth checking the nearby rough ground and gardens which flank the course in fall conditions (**6**). Hoopoe has been seen here.

The sea can be good for Eider flocks in late summer, which include the occasional King Eider. In spring, there are large numbers of Red-throated Divers offshore. Toward the north end of the links there is a bench where it is possible to look out over the beach and sea. A number of duck species use the area offshore. This is one of the better spots for scoters, which start to form large moulting flocks from June onwards and often include at least one Surf Scoter.

2. NORTH OF ABERDEEN

Blackdog to Drums

Blackdog (NJ 965 141)

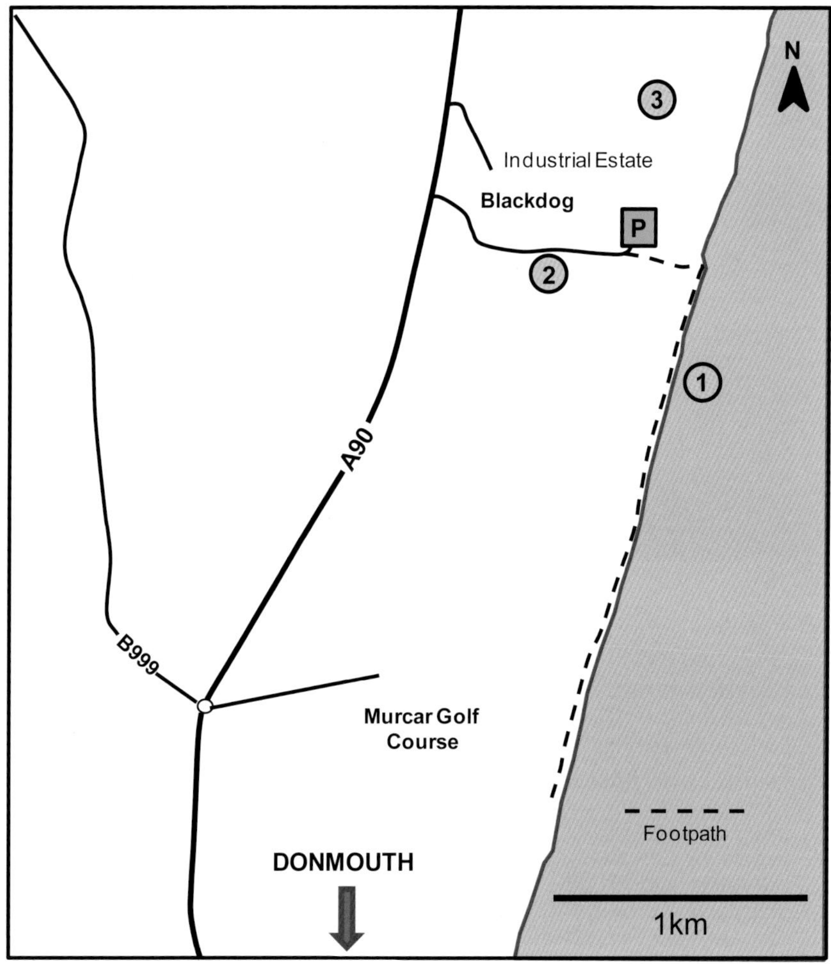

Location & access: Best accessed by turning off the A90, signposted to Blackdog (first Blackdog sign to the right), and follow the road (Hareburn Terrace) to the end. A rough track leads north to a car park. Do not drive or walk down to the house at the end of this track. Walk back to the gate and follow the track down to the sea, where scoters are usually found offshore from June until September, mainly to the south near Blackdog Rock (**1**) or further south towards Murcar Golf Course. Any areas of scrub at Blackdog should be checked, such as the trees east of the lane to the waterworks (**2**) or bushes on the rifle range (**3**).

Habitat and potential wildlife: The large Common Scoter flock builds up over the summer (June to September), with numbers reaching low thousands, along with tens, occasionally low hundreds of Velvets. Surf Scoters are regular, and recently both Black and White-winged Scoters have been found. Red-necked Grebe has been seen, along with large numbers of Eiders (many from the Sands of Forvie colony), the occasional King Eider, plus numerous Red-throated Divers. Sea-watching can turn up skuas, pursuing passing terns and loitering close to shore. The bushes and the gully at the car park and on the way down to Blackdog are always worth checking during fall conditions, and visible migration can be good here. The dunes at Blackdog are good for Six-spot Burnet, Dark Green Fritillary and Grayling.

Surf Scoter *N. Littlewood*

King Eider *N. Littlewood*

It is possible to walk south, along the dunes past Blackdog Rock (**1**), to **Murcar Golf Course**. The whole stretch of the coast is excellent for sea-duck, divers, terns and gulls (some large numbers can roost here). In the autumn, visible migration can be very evident, with many birds following the line of the coast or the line of dunes.

Balmedie Country Park (NJ 977 181)

Location & access: Turn off the A90 about ten kilometres north of Aberdeen into Balmedie. Follow the signs through the village to the beach and country park where parking and toilets are available.

Habitat and potential wildlife: A pleasant area to visit at any time of year with its vast dunes and beach. During spring and autumn though, this area has plenty to offer the visiting birder. The whole car park complex is well vegetated and the southern car park (by the toilet block) provides areas of long grass with a long line of willow to work through. One and a half kilometres north of the main car park between the dunes and fields is an area of wet willow scrub which, although extensive, is not too dense to work properly. A range of common and more unusual migrants have been found here over the years. Although disturbed,

Dark Green Fritillary *M. Sullivan*

the beach can be good for Sanderling, and offshore a similar range of birds to those of Blackdog can be found.

In summer a good variety of butterflies can be found here, including Dark Green Fritillary and Grayling, while Sandwich Terns, skuas and other sea birds can be seen offshore. Breeding Stonechats, Linnets and Meadow Pipits use the dunes.

Drums (NJ 997 221)

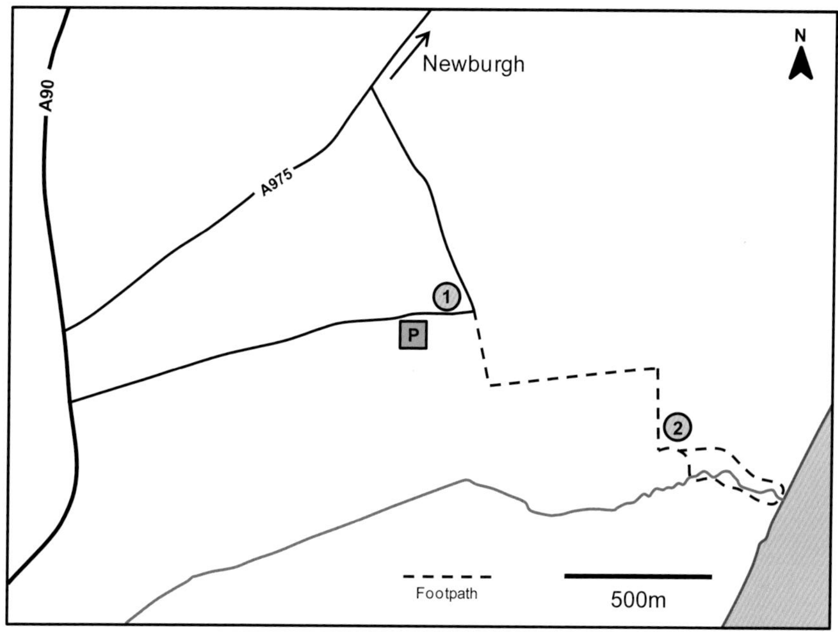

Location & access: From the A90 the safest access is to take the A975 to Newburgh, and turn right after 1.5km on the unclassified road signposted to Drums. *Access is very sensitive at this site, and visiting birders are urged to follow these instructions whilst being courteous to the local residents.*

Do not park at Drums farm (**1**) instead follow the tarmac road, turning right, around the corner of the farm garden, heading back towards the A92. After 50m there is a lay-by which can be used for parking. If residents of the cottages are available, please ask permission to park. On foot, walk from the farm buildings, heading south along the dirt track, which after c. 50m, goes past a cottage on the left, then turns left towards the sea. Follow this track between the fields to its end at a shooting range (**2**).

Habitat and potential wildlife: A few scattered bushes and trees with an understory of willowherb provide cover for migrant birds in the autumn. Follow the burn inland checking the willow and the gorse-covered banks. These can often produce good numbers of birds in the right conditions. The area has produced birds such as Pallas's Warbler in autumn, and recently, Booted Warbler. Spring passage can also be good. Watch for wheatears, finches and buntings in the fields on the way to the sea.

Around the Ythan Estuary

The Ythan Estuary and surrounding area is one of the best birding locations in the region. Good birds can be found throughout the year, but the estuary is particularly exciting in the early autumn (waders) and during the winter (wildfowl) when the number of birds on the Ythan can be daunting. However, the variety of habitats and the list of rarities found on the estuary illustrate the reward for patient scrutiny. A whole weekend could be dedicated to birding this large and varied area.

Ythan Estuary *F. Sullivan*

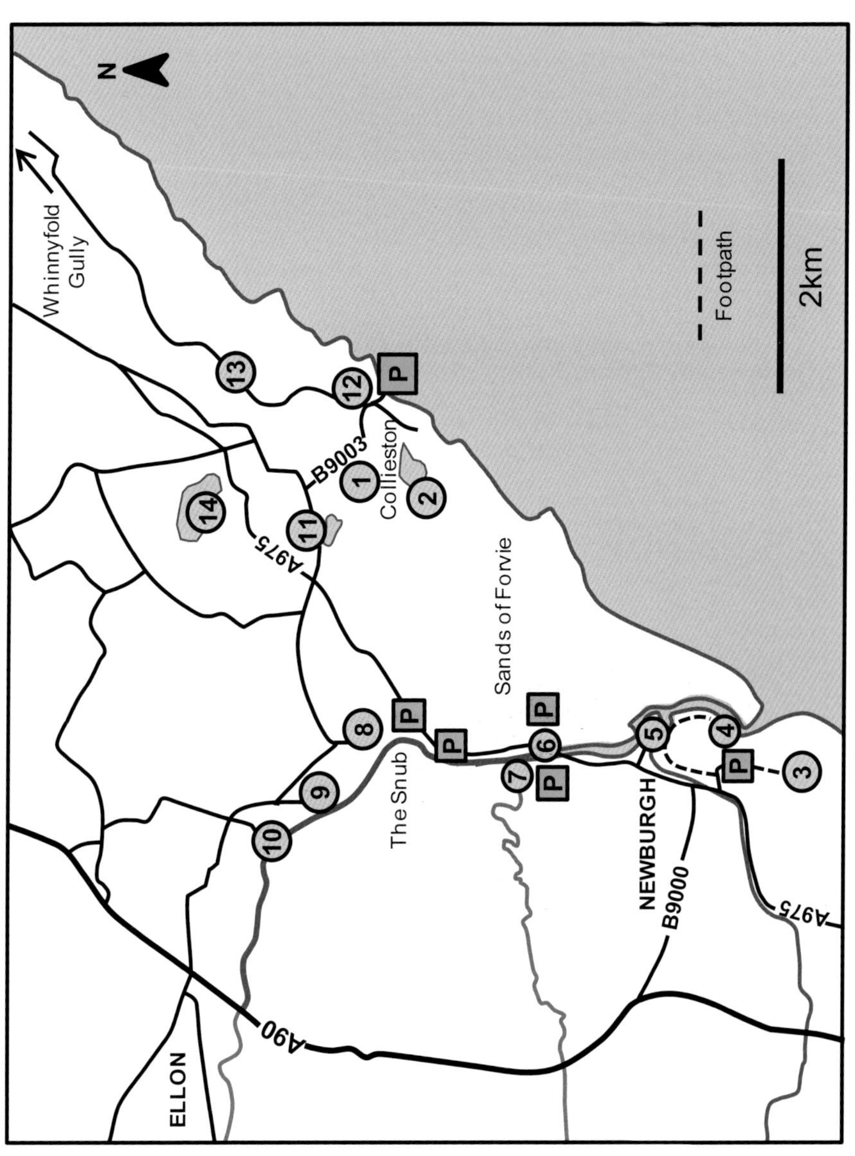
N
Whinnyfold
Gully
Collieston
B9003
A975
Sands of Forvie
The Snub
NEWBURGH
B9000
A90
ELLON
Footpath
2km
P
1
2
3
4
5
6
7
8
9
10
11
12
13
14

Sands of Forvie and the Ythan Estuary NNR

Location & access: A Scottish Natural Heritage **visitor centre** is located at **NK 034 289** (**1**) (Tel: 01358 751330) and can be accessed off the B9003 between Cotehill Loch and Collieston. Information regarding current sightings can be obtained here, and trail leaflets of the reserve are available.

From here, footpaths extend southwards into the moorland reserve and to **Sand Loch** (**NK 034 284**) (**2**) and the coast.

The estuary itself is too large to cover on foot. However, there are a number of access and viewing points, and probably the best strategy is to drive between these, then explore each on foot.

Starting at the south end of Newburgh village (food at the Udny Arms and Newburgh Hotel), drive to the car park at **NK 002 247** (access via Beach Road adjacent to the Newburgh Hotel). It is possible to walk south into the dunes and to the **Foveran bushes** (**NK 002 237**) (**3**) or north to the **Fishing huts** at **NK 004 247** (**4**) from where it is possible to view the estuary mouth and the ternery on the opposite bank. A circular walk, skirting the golf course, gives the opportunity to see a wide range of habitats and species. A tin hut (**NK 005 251**) half way around this walk is a good vantage point to look for waders, terns and gulls. A large haul-out of seals, (both Grey and Common and largest in summer) has developed on the north bank at the river mouth, and is a magnificent sight.

Little Tern *M. Sullivan*

Common Seals *M. Sullivan*

Inch Road at the north end of the village is a convenient place to check the mouth of Foveran Burn while **Inch Point** (**NK 004 256**) (**5**) provides good views of the mudflats up and downstream on the main River Ythan. Waders can be seen at close quarters here, and Little Egrets are fairly regular.

King Eider has historically been associated with Inch Point and the eider flocks are always worth checking, especially between April and July.

At **Waterside Bridge** (**6**) two car parks (**NK 001 268** and **NK 004 270**) provide access to the central and southern parts of the estuary. From the northern car park, signed footpaths extend alongside the estuary and across the dune and heathland areas. The eider and tern breeding areas are out of bounds (and largely out of view) during the summer but a footpath system provides access to other parts of the reserve.

From the southern car park (on the Newburgh side of the river), it is possible to walk upstream to investigate the Tarty Burn (**7**), which holds feeding and roosting waders, and which can be particularly good for freshwater species such as Green Sandpiper and has recorded a Long-billed Dowitcher.

Little Egret *M. Sullivan*

The middle section of the estuary is also viewable from lay-bys at **NK 003 281** and **NK 006 283**. **Inch Geck Island** (**NJ 999 278**) attracts roosting waders at high tide and many of the estuary's rarities have been seen on the island at one time or another. Little Egrets regularly use this area for feeding.

Waulkmill hide (**NK 003 290**) (**8**) provides good views across the upper estuary. Follow the A975 northwards. Turn left at the Collieston crossroads onto the B9003, and follow the road downhill to the river. Just before a bridge there is a track on the left leading to the hide and a parking area. Large numbers of waders and gulls can be present in front of the hide. The estuary and surrounding fields hold large numbers of grey geese during passage times, with smaller numbers during winter. Ospreys can be numerous here in late summer - check the fence posts on the south side of the river. The hide faces south-west, so morning visits tend to allow better viewing conditions.

Fisherman's Car Park (**NJ 996 294**) (**9**) gives access to the upper reaches of the estuary, and allows views of the large gull and wader flocks that are often just visible from Waulkmill hide. On leaving Waulkmill turn left, and follow the road to where a track to the left is reached, just before a steep right-hand bend. Follow the track downhill and the car parking area is at the end of the track. Park sensibly in the small car park, and walk down to the small angling club hut, from where the flocks can be scoped.

Logie Buchan Bridge (**NJ 991 299**) (**10**) is the most upstream of the regularly watched points on the estuary. Leaving the Fisherman's area turn left, and continue until a crossroad is reached. Take the first left and follow the road down (bearing right at a junction) to the bridge (closed to traffic). Here the Ythan narrows and passes upstream through a small reed bed. Water Rail is regular here, along with other freshwater marsh specialities (including a large late summer swallow roost), and Bearded Tits have been recorded.

Ringing here turns up rarities, including Blyth's Reed and Paddyfield Warblers.

Paddyfield Warbler *P. Crockett*

Blyth's Reed Warbler *P. Crockett*

Habitat and potential wildlife: The National Nature Reserve covers just over 1,000 hectares and is managed by Scottish Natural Heritage and includes the Ythan Estuary as well as dune, heath and moorland areas. The reserve is of significant botanical interest and supports internationally important numbers of breeding terns (with four species) and a nationally significant Eider colony (up to 5,000 birds), as well as thousands of wintering waders, ducks and geese.

Common Eider *M. Sullivan*

Although most notable for its breeding birds other species can be found during the year on Forvie. Snow Buntings and Twite are present in winter, often commuting between the sands and the dunes around Foveran bushes. The areas of the reserve that are dotted with bushes can hold migrant passerines in spring and autumn. Sand Loch holds small numbers of common duck and occasional migrants. During most winters this is an excellent site to see Short-eared Owl hunting around the loch margins in the afternoon. The dunes occasionally attract Rough-legged Buzzard in winter.

On the river, Ospreys are regular in summer and, prior to autumn migration, 6-8 may be seen fishing or sitting on posts along the river. Marsh Harriers often pass through (and have bred in the area). A wide range of waders use the estuary on passage and in winter; anything can, and does, turn up.

The woodland and scrub (especially the inter-dune scrublands) are attractive to passerine migrants. Regular ringing at Foveran bushes has turned up a wide range of rare migrants.

Cotehill Loch (NK 027 293)

Location & access: Turn right off the A975 about 5km north of Newburgh onto the B9003 road signposted to Collieston. The loch (**11**) is visible from the road and it is suggested that a rapid scan of the loch be made from the road. Please do not block any of the driveways to the houses.

Habitat and potential wildlife: This small loch holds numbers of commoner ducks and sometimes Whooper Swans. It is always worth a quick scan when in the area as it has turned up a few rarities over the years. It used to be good for waders (Wilson's Phalarope has been recorded here), but these days the water levels are usually too high to attract them.

Collieston (NK 042 286)

Location & access: The small coastal village of Collieston lies approximately 4km north of the Ythan Estuary. When visiting Collieston, parking can be tricky and it is best to park at Cransdale car park, on your left just as you enter the village. Local birders are on good terms with the villagers, but please respect the residents whose gardens you peer into, and of course, the churchyard.

Habitat and potential wildlife: The village is primarily known as an area for coastal migrants during the spring and autumn and is a favoured site where many local and national rarities have been found. Some of the best known areas are as you enter the village, the willows and sycamores by the churchyard (**12**), as well as in the churchyard itself and the gully leading down to the sea. However, just about any sheltered garden or patch of rank vegetation is worth checking in the right conditions and nearly all are easily viewable from public paths.

Yellow-browed Warbler *P. Crockett*

Although Collieston is primarily a migrant site, sea-watching from the Cransdale viewpoint can also be productive with skuas and shearwaters regularly recorded. Puffins breed locally, and can be seen on the sea, with other auks, Kittiwake and Fulmar, from the viewpoint in summer. It is always worth checking the fields on the approach to Collieston, and those around the Collieston crossroads (**NK 021 294**), as these have regularly turned up Buff-breasted Sandpiper in the early autumn.

Passing cetaceans in summer add interest, with regular Bottlenose Dolphin and Harbour Porpoise. Killer Whale has been seen in the past few summers and may be becoming more regular.

Driving north from Collieston on the single track road at the churchyard signposted for Whinnyfold, a couple of small wooded areas known as the **"Whinnyfold Plantation"** (**13**) can be found around **NK 04 30**. Please park carefully in the field gate leaving room for vehicles to pass. Pallas's Grasshopper Warbler was found here in September 2012.

Meikle Loch RSPB Reserve (NK 029 308)

Location & access: Seven kilometres north of Newburgh on the A975 and about 200 metres before reaching Slains Primary School, there is an unmarked track to the left. Drive this slowly. At the end of the short track lies Meikle Loch (**14**), the largest loch in the area. The loch itself is an RSPB reserve, bought to protect the large Pink-footed Goose roost. Birders should, as always, park sensibly, not disturb the wildfowl and not walk around the loch edge. Check any temporary pools adjacent to the A975 and side roads ("Slains Pools") which have attracted waders on passage.

Habitat and potential wildlife: The loch supports a good variety of wildfowl throughout the year and impressive numbers (up to 20,000) of Pink-footed Geese roost there in the autumn. The loch is always worth a visit as there are continuous changes in the wildfowl present. Ringed-necked Duck with the flock of Tufted Duck was regular in 2014. Unusual grebes and wildfowl occur in winter, as do marsh terns and Little Gulls on passage. Raptors including Marsh Harrier and White-tailed Eagle (from the Fife re-introduction project) can sometimes be seen here, as can Ospreys. During wader passage the shoreline can be very productive, especially when water levels are low.

Pectoral Sandpiper
P. Crockett

Haddo House and Country Park (NJ 868 347)

This site, inland from the rest in this section, allows a glimpse of the farmland and woodland birds to be found on the Buchan Plain.

Location & access: North-west of Ellon up the Ythan valley lies Haddo – an old estate now managed as a country park with the house maintained by the National Trust for Scotland. Follow the A920 westwards from Ellon turning right onto the B999.The main entrance lies just north of Tarves at **NJ 875 324**. There is a large car park and coffee shop by the house.

Habitat and potential wildlife: Two ornamental lochs are found here, surrounded by parkland trees, many very old, holding some rare lichens. There is a wide range of wildfowl here (including Teal, Goosander and Goldeneye), some "tame" (though most are wild), which allow close views. The loch used to hold a Greylag Goose roost, though the birds present here now are from feral stock. Ospreys can be seen fishing here and the old trees hold Stock Doves and a wide range of woodland birds. Red Squirrels can easily be seen here, especially around the wildlife garden near the car park. Otters can be seen on the loch.

Cruden Bay to Peterhead

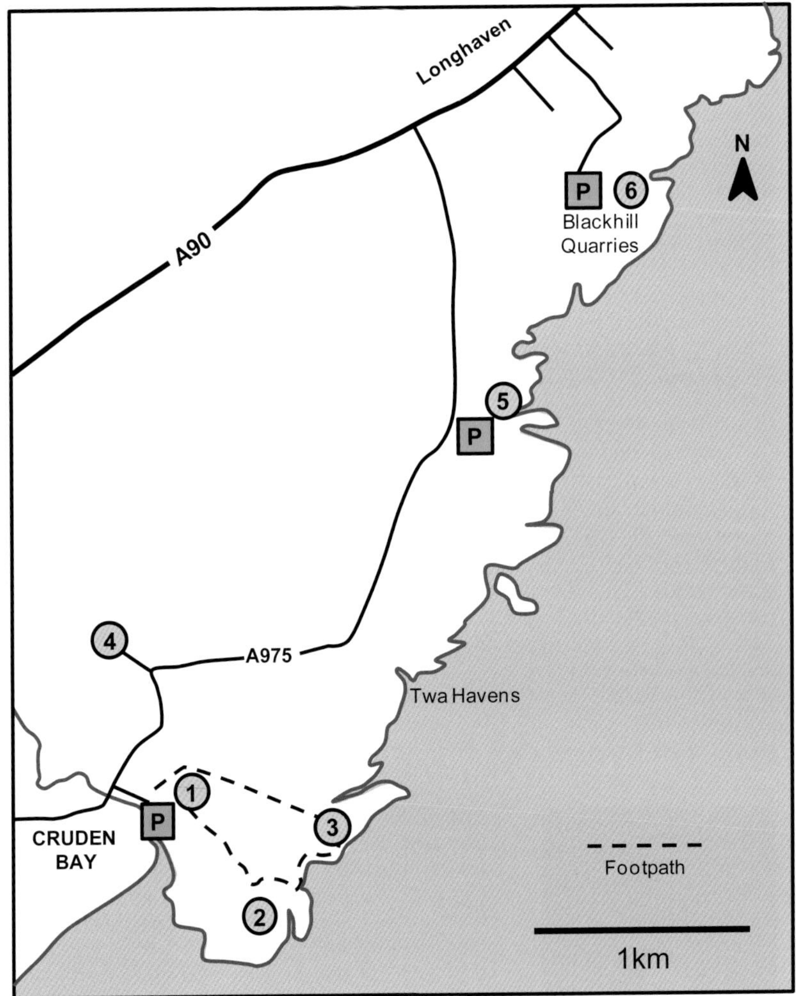

Cruden Bay Woods (NK 094 364)

Location & access: Cruden Bay is on the A975 between Peterhead and Newburgh. The bay itself can hold small numbers of waders such as Sanderling and Ringed Plover, with much larger numbers of gulls and terns often present at the southern end. Cruden Bay Woods are reached by taking the harbour road opposite the Kilmarnock Arms Hotel (excellent bar meals). Past the shops there is a car park on the left. From the car park, follow the path through the woods, searching the willows along the stream. At the eastern end the path follows the cliffs to Slains Castle, at the edge of cultivated fields. A track from the castle heads back to Cruden Bay and the car park through fields and some mature woodland.

Habitat and potential wildlife: Cruden Bay has the most extensive area of cover on this stretch of coast, with mature Sycamore woodland and willows running alongside the burn. Migrants may be seen anywhere in the woods but they are usually present in good numbers beyond the footbridge over the burn (**1**). This patch of willows can be very productive, especially for Pallas's and Yellow-browed Warblers in autumn. Further down the valley there is a brick tower on the left (**2**), in this area there is a variety of trees and bushes with the burn running through them. This general area can be productive for migrants (has included Long-eared Owls roosting in the trees). Continuing up the path towards Slains Castle (**3**), it is worth checking the stubble fields as this is one of North-East Scotland's more regular sites for Lapland Buntings. Grey Partridge is also regular here.

Long-eared Owl
M. Sullivan

Nearby is the old **Cruden Bay Brickworks** (**NK 088 370**). Follow the A975 north out of Cruden Bay and at a very sharp right-hand bend take the minor road to the left (signposted to Auchiries). Pull into a lay-by (**4**) on the left at the obvious old industrial site. The brick pits now form a series of ponds with breeding Tufted Duck and Little Grebe. Large numbers of dabbling duck can gather here in winter and are always worth checking for rarer species. The old spoil tips are covered by scrub holding breeding Whitethroat and Sedge Warbler. A Subalpine Warbler was found here in 2013.

Bullers of Buchan (NK 107 380)

Guillemot *M. Sullivan*

Location & access: Situated between Cruden Bay and Peterhead, 'the Bullers' are reached by taking the A975 signposted north of Cruden Bay (**5**). An obvious car park, just south of a dismantled railway bridge, on the east of the road has an information board. To view the birds take the path by the houses and walk north along the cliff top.

Habitat and potential wildlife: The Bullers of Buchan is one of the best and easiest places to see nesting seabirds (May-July) in North-East Scotland. There are thousands of Guillemots and Kittiwakes with smaller numbers of Razorbills, Puffins, Shags and Fulmars. In the spring and autumn the gardens around the houses often have small numbers of migrants with Pied Flycatchers and Redstarts seen annually.

Longhaven Cliffs (NK 114 394)

Location & access: A Scottish Wildlife Trust cliff top reserve (**6**), access is via a poorly maintained track on the east side of the A90 just north of the village of Longhaven. At the end of the track there is a car park by a ruined cottage. The area is one of old granite quarries, with pools, coastal heathland and the sea cliffs. A well-marked footpath leads along the cliff top.

Habitat and potential wildlife: a variety of habitats exist, with grazing land (with breeding Lapwing), scrub and an overgrown garden, water-filled quarries and the cliffs. Migrants have been found here, but the area is more important for breeding birds. Auks, including Puffin, together with Kittiwake and Shag breed on the cliffs, and Tufted Duck and Kestrel nest in the quarries. Gulls use the fresh water to bathe, with large numbers loafing around.

Kittiwake *M. Sullivan*

Peterhead (NK 136 460)

Location & access: Peterhead is known for its winter gulls, attracted by the town's fishing fleet. The harbour area is quite large and perhaps best explored by car; simply drive around looking for gulls. Harbour Street and the fish processing sheds (**1+2**) are a good place to start. Grey Seals can be seen well in the harbour.

North of the harbour lies **Buchanhaven**, where the rocky shoreline along Gadel Braes (**NK 131 469**) (**3**) provides excellent views of waders on red granite at high tide.

Habitat and potential wildlife: Birds often gather on the large buildings at **NK 137 458** (**Scott's Pier**) or, at low tide, in the rocks at **NK 127 456** (off the A982 South Rd). Glaucous and Iceland Gulls are regularly encountered during the winter, with birds occasionally summering. There are often passing seabirds offshore (regular counts of thousands of birds moving in the right conditions, plus rarer species - even a Frigatebird sp. flew past here in 2010!).

Glaucous Gull *C. Gibbins*

Northwards the rocky shoreline, best accessed from Gadel Braes, allows views of the bay, with sea-watching possibilities (divers and grebes, occasionally including Red-necked), and Purple Sandpiper and Turnstone feeding or roosting close to the road.

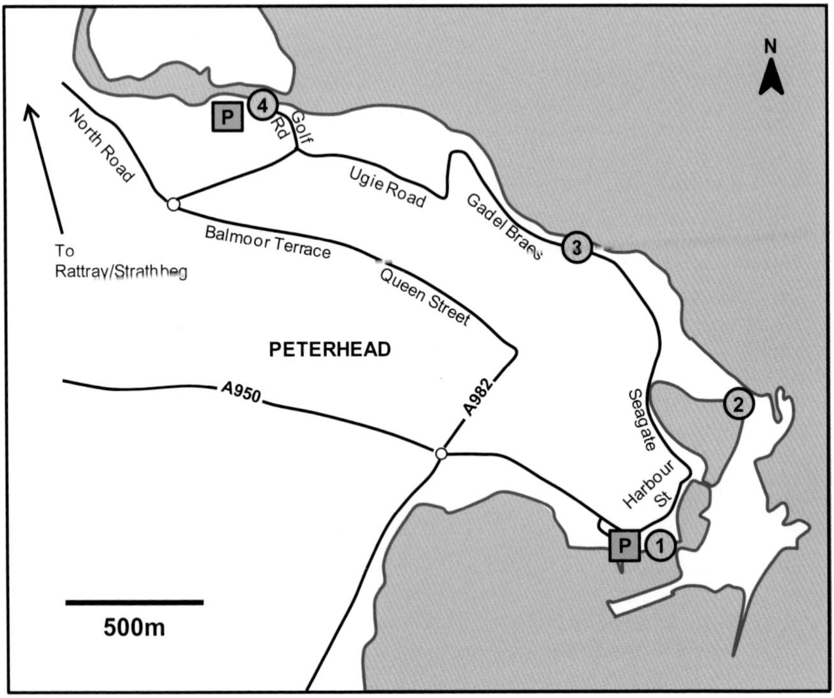

River Ugie Estuary (NK 121 473)

Location & access: The estuary of the River Ugie is quite small and is easily checked from a car park on the northern edge of Peterhead where the river enters the sea (**4**). Follow Golf Road (off Ugie Road) down to the car park.

Habitat and potential wildlife: From the car park, a footpath extends upriver for c. 500m and provides an excellent vantage for viewing gulls, sea-duck and passage waders. The footpath also extends seaward and joins the promenade at **NK 123 473**. From here it is possible to check the gulls and terns on the beach. Very close views of confiding Turnstone can be had here in winter. Passage and wintering Short-eared Owls can frequent the adjacent golf course.

Ugie Estuary *I. Francis*

3. THE NORTH COAST OF ABERDEENSHIRE

The stretch of coast west from Rattray Head includes some of the finest birding in our area. This includes wintering gulls in Fraserburgh, to breeding sea-birds (including one of only two British mainland colonies of Gannets, at Troup Head), and migrant hotspots such as Rattray Head. In addition, the magnificent RSPB reserve at the Loch of Strathbeg, with its wintering geese and Whooper Swans, thousands of ducks, summering Marsh Harriers, regular Pectoral Sandpiper among many passage waders, and breeding duck, warblers and waders (not to mention regular records of Bearded Tit and Bittern) is a "must visit".

Around the Loch of Strathbeg

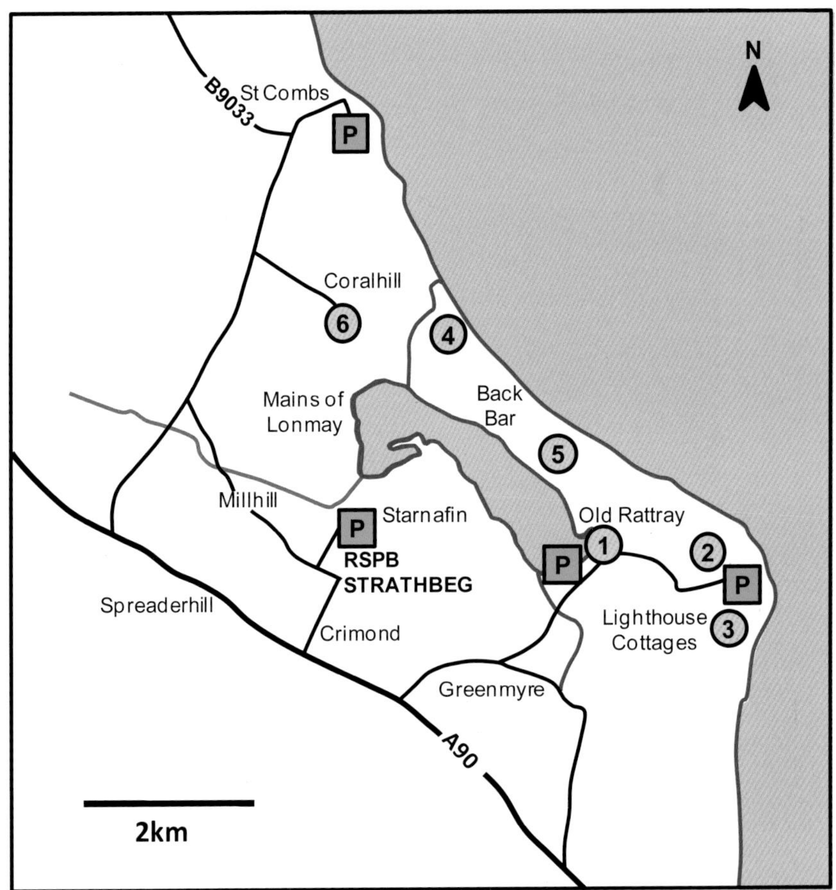

Rattray Head (NK 104 577)

Location & access: Rattray Head is one of North-East Scotland's best known migration sites and is reached by turning off the A90 Peterhead to Fraserburgh road, just north of St. Fergus, signposted to Rattray. The road passes the southern end of the Loch of Strathbeg where there is a parking area by the ruined church; this allows views over the south of the Loch and is also a good place to see Corn Buntings (**1**). The road gets very rough beyond this car park, so proceed with caution. Follow the road until it ends at the houses (Lighthouse Cottages) by the dunes, where there is a rough car park.

Habitat and potential wildlife: Rattray consists of a sandy beach with some rocky outcrops; backed by extensive sand dunes and grazed fields. From

Rattray Head "floods" and dunes *I. Francis*

autumn to spring there are often some areas of open water, one of which, the 'floods', is in the field adjacent to the parking area by the houses (**2**). The other pool, (the 'flashes') is between Rattray and St. Fergus gas terminal and can be seen from the gorse-covered mound by the houses looking southwards. It is reached by walking along the fence line behind the dunes; a telescope is needed as it is difficult to approach closely without flushing the birds. The 'flashes' are good for waders, and ducks such as Garganey are regular in spring when water is present. The 'floods' adjacent to the parking area are very good for waders; Little Stint, Curlew Sandpiper and Ruff are regular visitors, while Temminck's Stint, Green-winged Teal, Little Gull, White-winged Black Tern and Garganey have also been seen.

In spring there is very little cover and, if there are no birds to be seen around the gorse-covered mound or in the gardens, then further investigation is unlikely to produce much. The lack of cover means that if migrants are present they are easy to see. The best time for migrants is around the first two weeks of May when Bluethroats, Red-backed Shrikes and Wrynecks should be searched for.

Red-breasted Flycatcher
T. Marshall

In autumn, nettles, burdock and dock provide more cover especially in the field south of the houses (**3**). September and October are the best months, with Yellow-browed Warbler, Barred Warbler and Red-breasted Flycatcher being almost annual. A long-staying Desert Wheatear spent the winter on the beach here in 2012-2013.

Rattray is also a good sea-watching site, although it is a little exposed. Walk north from the car park and follow the obvious paths through the dunes to access the shore. In autumn Manx Shearwater, Arctic and Great Skuas are regular while Pomarine Skuas and Sooty Shearwater can be seen most years. During the winter there are sometimes over 5,000 Eiders with good numbers of Long-tailed Ducks and some Common Scoters. Little Auks may also be seen in the winter. Late winter and early spring is a good time to look for Great Northern Diver, another Rattray special with groups of tens of birds occurring.

Gt. Northern Diver *M. Sullivan*

Loch of Strathbeg RSPB Reserve (NK 057 580)

Loch of Strathbeg *D. Goulder*

Location & access: From the A90 in the village of Crimond, take the right turn beside the Kirk, following the brown tourist sign to the reserve. At the T-junction at the end of the road, turn left. After approximately 500 m, turn right at the reserve entrance sign onto the entrance track and follow the track to the car park. Four hides are available, and a map of the reserve is available at the visitor centre. This will give up to date directions for the hides (Fen and Bay) on the Loch itself. Currently it is necessary to drive south-east on the A90 and follow signs for Crimond Airfield before following RSPB signs around the edge of the old airfield. During summer, a footpath is available from the visitor centre to the loch-side hides. The reserve is one of the premier wildlife sites in North-East Scotland, and a full day in and around the reserve will be worthwhile at any time of the year.

Loch of Strathbeg Pink-footed Geese *F. Sullivan*

Habitat and potential wildlife: The reserve is a mixture of the loch itself and its surrounding reed-beds, re-flooded agricultural land at the western end (the "Low Ground"), small areas of woodland and fields now growing cover crops for wintering seed-eating birds. Check the gardens and feeders at the visitor centre where a wide range of birds, including a large population of Tree Sparrows is to be found. A Steppe Grey Shrike has been found here, and the trees regularly attract spring and autumn migrants.

On the north side it is possible to access the sand-dunes and beach, along with the outflow from the loch, which forms an intra-dune lagoon during high water levels. The wide range of habitats, along with the reserve's location ensures a variety of species. Wildfowl form the most important group with large numbers (sometimes up to 65,000) of Pink-footed Geese from September to March, along with wintering Whooper Swans (several hundred). Rarer geese can be found when scanning through the large flocks. Dabbling duck are regularly present in large numbers in winter, with Wigeon, Teal and Mallard forming the bulk, with smaller numbers of Pintail, Shoveler and Gadwall also present. Among the duck flocks regular American Wigeon and Green-winged Teal are found. Diving ducks are also to be found with Goldeneye, Tufted Duck and Pochard all present, along with occasional Scaup. Sawbills include occasional wintering Smew. Grebes (including regular wintering Slavonian) can be found on the Loch.

The reed-beds usually hold wintering Bittern each year and often Bearded Tit (which bred in 2014), and are quartered by Marsh Harrier in summer and by wintering Hen Harriers.

Tree Sparrow *M. Sullivan*

The Low Ground is managed as a feeding and roosting area for the wintering geese, but it is also a magnet for waders with a range of species present most of the year, and vagrants regularly found. The Low Ground must be one of the UK's most regular sites for Pectoral Sandpiper, and they displayed here in spring 2004.

The scrubby loch-side woodland holds the expected range of breeding birds, and can attract migrants. A large rookery is present on the reserve. The cover crop attracts large numbers of birds in winter, with 90 or more Corn Buntings, along with hundreds of Yellowhammers, with Reed Bunting and mixed finch flocks (which sometimes attract birds of prey). The area is also a stronghold for Tree Sparrow, with good numbers around the feeders at the visitor centre car park, where they also breed.

The visitor centre (with views across the Low Ground), and the Tower Pool Hide (Low Ground and Savoch) are accessed from the main reserve car park.

Otter *M. Sullivan*

The Fen Hide is the best placed to see wintering Bittern and Bearded Tit, as well as one of the most regular places to see Otter.

Buff-breasted Sandpiper *M. Sullivan*

The dunes give access to the sea and the **lagoon** (**4**), both attracting a range of birds (including Buff-breasted Sandpiper and Lesser Yellowlegs in 2014), while the **plantation** (**5**) in the dunes forms a migration hot spot attracting large numbers of birds on spring and autumn passage. These are accessible from **Coralhill** (**6**), but please be careful while parking, and don't block access.

St. Combs (NK 056 630)

Location & access: St. Combs is a small seaside village situated halfway between the well-watched birding sites of Rattray Head and Kinnaird Head (Fraserburgh). The area around St. Combs is under-watched but potentially could produce good birds at any time of the year. Approaching from Peterhead on the A90, take the right turn along the B9033 (2km past the village of Crimond, signposted St. Combs). Follow this road all the way through the village towards the sea. Just after a sharp right-hand bend in the road, turn towards the Tufted Duck Hotel and park. The beach can be reached by taking the path down what is an old fossil cliff and across the dunes. A walk north along the beach towards Inverallochy can be very pleasant given a nice day. Food is available at the Tufted Duck Hotel.

Habitat and potential wildlife: St. Combs is situated on an extensive dune system that extends south to Peterhead and north (albeit mostly in the form of golf courses) to Fraserburgh. The shoreline is made up of sandy beach interspersed with rocky outcrops that are exposed at low tide and attract good numbers of waders. Scanning the sea from the car park can be particularly productive in winter with Red-throated and Great Northern Divers, Scaup, Common Scoter, Long-tailed Duck, Red-breasted Merganser and Little Auk all possible. Skuas, shearwaters and petrels can be seen in small numbers in late summer. The surrounding fields attract large numbers of wintering passerines with flocks of 100+ Corn Buntings having been recorded in the past. A trip of Dotterel has occasionally been located in fields just south of the village in May. There are small patches of scrubby vegetation and trees around the village which attract migrants. Offshore there are records of a range of cetaceans, including Minke Whales, and Basking Sharks have been sighted here in the past few summers.

Minke Whale *I. Francis*

Cairnbulg, Inverallochy (NK 04 65)

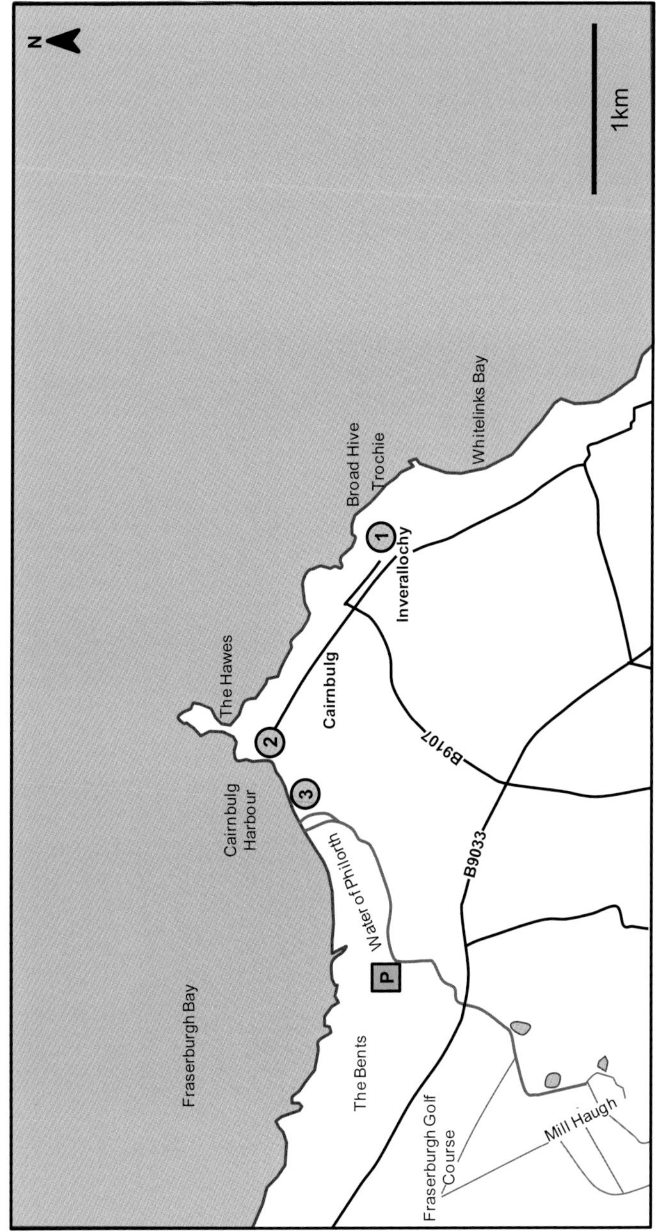

Location & access: Cairnbulg and Inverallochy are two adjoining, coastal villages situated on the east side of Fraserburgh Bay. Coming from Peterhead, just before reaching the village of St. Combs, turn left at the crossroads to stay on the B9033 to Fraserburgh. After about 2km turn right onto the B9107 which leads into the two villages. At the end of the road, either turn right and follow the road along the edge of the golf course, parking at the Scottish Water pump-house (**1**) or head north for the car park at Cairnbulg Harbour (**2**), which is easily reached if you remain on the road you came in on, negotiating the roundabout and sleeping policemen en route. The shoreline between Inverallochy and Cairnbulg can then be explored either by car or on foot. The sandy bay at the harbour collects seaweed, attracting a wide range of waders and other birds, which feast on flies breeding in the rotting weed. Just west of the harbour lies the mouth of the **Water of Philorth** (**3**) and the local nature reserve. This can be accessed on foot from Cairnbulg Harbour, or from the car park at **NK 021 649**.

Habitat and potential wildlife: The extensive rocky foreshore and the sandy beach at Cairnbulg Harbour attract large numbers of waders from late summer and through the winter. A good diversity of species has been recorded including both godwits, Curlew Sandpiper, Little Stint and Jack Snipe. A considerable number of gulls collect at the mouth of the Water of Philorth just to the west of the harbour and, during the winter, regularly includes Glaucous and Iceland Gulls. Attracted by the feast of waders, Peregrine and Merlin can often be seen darting through the feeding flocks. Often, large numbers of Starlings forage noisily amongst the piled-up mounds of kelp. A Spotted Sandpiper was present on the rocks just south of Inverallochy from October 2014 into 2015.

Black-tailed and Bar-tailed Godwits
M. Sullivan

Dunlin *M. Sullivan*

Fraserburgh to Portsoy

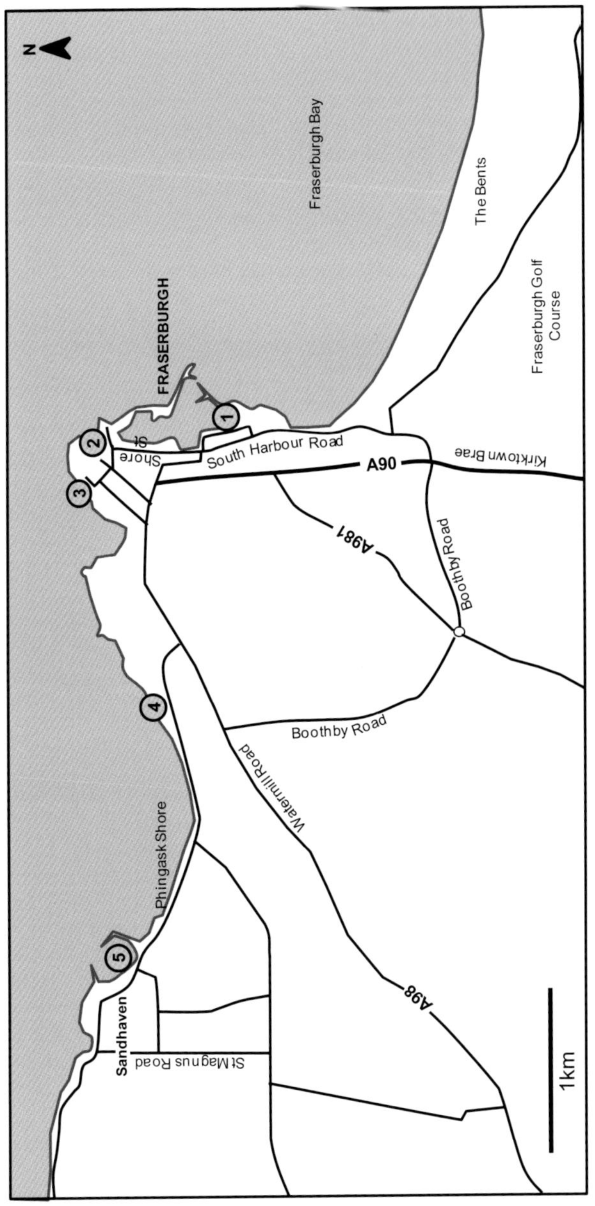

Kinnaird Head (NJ 997 676) and Fraserburgh Harbour (NJ 997 676)

Location & access: On entering Fraserburgh, head for the harbour (**1**) (via South Harbour and Harbour roads). Park and search the harbour area for gulls (sliced white bread is a great attractant for gulls and Grey Seals!). Having checked the harbour, proceed northwards on Shore St. to Bath St. Turn right and on the left there is a rough car park overlooking Kinnaird Head and the sea (**2**). It is possible to sea-watch from the car here. Alternatively, continue to the Lighthouse Museum (follow signage) and sea-watch from there (**3**).

Habitat and potential wildlife: One of Scotland's premier sea-watching points. Gulls are abundant around the headland and the harbour, where numerous white-winged gulls are almost always present in winter and often in summer too.

Iceland (left) and Kumlein's Gulls (right) *M. Sullivan*

Ross's Gulls (including three together) were recorded in the 1980s and 90s. Late summer (July - August) is proving to be a good time to see numbers of Storm Petrels just off the rocks, along with post-breeding flocks of Black Guillemot. Passerine migrants are also frequent here. Black Redstarts have been seen sheltering in the buildings and small hollows around the headland. Purple Sandpipers roost at Kinnaird Head and over 100 may be seen. Turnstones can be seen at close range on the harbour walls feeding on fish and crab waste. Improvements to the sewage system have probably removed the food source for birds, so opportunities for seeing the more unusual gulls are perhaps not as good as they were, however rare birds continue to turn up.

Phingask Bay (NJ 975 670) and Sandhaven (NJ 964 675) to Rosehearty (NJ 931 678)

Location & access: Westwards from Fraserburgh, small pull-ins for parking are available along the B9031 allowing access to the shore, and unrestricted parking is available around the Sandhaven and Rosehearty harbours.

Habitat and potential wildlife: Close to Fraserburgh large numbers of gulls wash, feed and roost along the shore, and on the roofs of the industrial units. From here to Rosehearty lies a fascinating stretch of coast with broad shelves of cobbles, rock pools and sand. This unusual coastline, including the stretch at Phingask shore (**4**), is more like western Scotland, with a width of several hundred metres of kelp-dominated pools and shingle. The area is a Site of Special Scientific Interest, both geologically and for its wintering birds.

It used to hold nationally important numbers of wintering Purple Sandpipers and Turnstones (perhaps 400–500 or more of each), but, in common with many sites in Britain, numbers have dropped markedly. However, there are still many thousands of birds on this stretch of coast. Large numbers of Redshank and Curlew are regular, together with a good mix of most other common winter and passage waders. Hundreds of ducks (mainly Eider, Wigeon, Mallard and Red-breasted Merganser) are offshore, along with many Red-throated Divers, Long-tailed Ducks and passing Gannets and auks. The wintering gull flocks almost always contain Glaucous and usually Iceland Gulls, and Mediterranean Gull is regular in winter especially in Sandhaven Harbour (**5**). Other rarer gulls are attracted to the large flocks of commoner species. A Laughing Gull was found along this stretch of coast in December 2012. Over 100 Rock Pipits have been counted along the shore here, and there is usually a good range of other passerines to be seen. These in turn attract raptors such as Peregrine and wintering Merlin, while Short-eared Owl hunt the shoreline and neighbouring fields. Just inland, the fields are worth checking in winter for scattered flocks of buntings. Parts of the area to the south of here have some of the densest Corn Bunting populations in the UK, with some large winter flocks.

Laughing Gull *T. Marshall*

Phingask Shore *I. Francis*

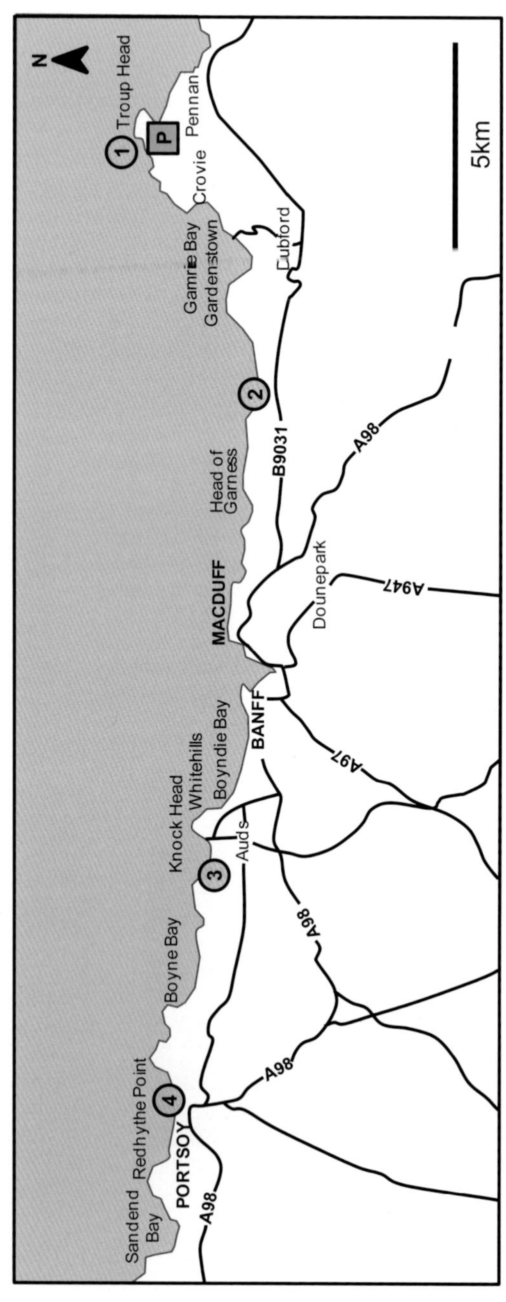
N
Troup Head
1
P
Pennan
Crovie
Gamrie Bay
Gardenstown
Cubford
2
B9031
A98
Head of Garness
MACDUFF
Dounepark
A947
BANFF
Boyndie Bay
Whitehills
A97
Knock Head
Auds
3
A98
Boyne Bay
Redhythe Point
4
A98
PORTSOY
Sandend Bay
A98
5km

Troup Head RSPB Reserve (NJ 822 665)

Location & access: Troup, Pennan and Lion Head Special Protection Area lies immediately east of Crovie and extends to the 'Local Hero' village of Pennan. Troup Head (**1**) is found between Pennan and Gardenstown on the B9031, east along the coast from Macduff. The RSPB nature reserve is signposted off the B9031 along with a sign for Northfield Farm. Follow the RSPB brown signs to Northfield Farm, drive through the farmyard and onto a rough track to the reserve car park. Park here and follow RSPB brown signs through a gate and along the fence line through the field. A track through the gorse leads to a gate, the main sea bird colony is on the left through this gate. Visitor boats also sail from Macduff during the summer, offering a unique view of the reserve. Try Puffin Cruises at www.puffincruises.com.

Troup Head *M. Sullivan*

Habitat and potential wildlife: This large seabird colony, of European importance, is spread over three main headlands, but the best to visit is Troup Head. Not only are the views of tens of thousands of Guillemots, hundreds of Razorbills and many Puffins spectacular, but this headland also holds the only colony of Gannets on the British mainland away from Flamborough Head. This colony was founded in 1988, and since then it has increased massively to over 2,800 pairs in 2013. Keep an eye out for passing seabirds and cetaceans too. The best period to visit is May to July, when the breeding season is at its height. Ravens and Peregrines are also

Gannets *M. Sullivan*

seen here regularly.

Spectacular wildflower displays also occur at this time. Spring Squill and Heath spotted Orchids are a major attraction of this reserve.

Spring Squill *M. Sullivan*

Heath spotted Orchid
F. Sullivan

Macduff (NJ 705 645)

Location & access: Situated on the A98, roughly halfway between Cullen and Fraserburgh.

Habitat and potential wildlife: At Macduff, adjacent to Banff, the Marine Life Aquarium (open all year) is a very successful attraction, as its entire stock of fish and marine organisms come from the Moray Firth. Improve your knowledge of the food web in the sea, and how it might affect birds! The RSPB has a presence here also, with information about the Troup Head reserve. Boat trips to Troup can be taken from the harbour (www.puffincruises.com).The coast east of Macduff along to Gardenstown is very little explored. Black Guillemots can be seen along to Stocked Head (**2**) (**NJ 755 646**) and breeding probably takes place. Otherwise, scattered Fulmars and other seabirds are found on these steep cliffs, with widespread breeding Rock Pipits, occasional Peregrines and increasingly Ravens, which now breed on the north coast.

Banff (NJ 685 645)

Location & access: Situated on the A98, roughly halfway between Cullen and Fraserburgh.

Habitat and potential wildlife: Banff Bay can hold large numbers of duck in winter, though fewer now that improvements have been made to the sewage treatment plant and the associated outfalls. The gulls are always worth checking along with the hundreds of Eiders. Goldeneye, sawbills and gulls can often be found close in. The River Deveron flows into the sea at Banff, and significant numbers of Goosanders and Goldeneye can be found.

The coastal strip from Banff to Portsoy still has Corn Buntings, with small winter flocks noted here, as well as scattered breeders singing on telephone wires, though Rosehearty is the best area for this species. The area around **Whitehills** (**3**) (**NJ 655 655**) is well worth exploring. Farmland here often holds numbers of Lapwings and Golden Plovers, and these, together with the frequently large flocks of finches and buntings, draw in Peregrine and Merlin, often seen in the autumn and winter. A scan offshore from Knock Head at Whitehills usually reveals a good passage of seabirds, especially Gannets, but also Sandwich Terns in summer. The raised beaches behind the caravan site off Harbour Place (NJ 660 658) are covered in scrub, and often hold migrants in conditions of north-easterly winds in autumn. It is worth making the point that all along this coast there are many small hollows, burnsides and scrub patches which in the right conditions are undoubtedly used by migrants every year, and many are under-watched.

Portsoy (NJ 590 662)

Location & access: Located off the A98, mid-way between Banff and Cullen (**4**). Follow the narrow Church St. downhill to the harbour where parking is available. A café

here is open year round.

Habitat and potential wildlife: Any journey along this north coast should include a brief stop in Portsoy, an ancient and attractive fishing village with a very interesting harbour. In recent years this has been a regular site for White-billed Diver, with up to 20 birds counted in spring along the coast from late March to mid-May as they moult from winter to breeding plumage. These birds can be seen from shore but are often very distant and are best viewed by boat, such as the Gemini Explorer, operated from Buckie, or Puffin Cruises from Macduff.

White-billed Diver *M. Sullivan*

4. THE COAST SOUTH OF ABERDEEN

Much of the coastline south of the city boundary offers huge potential for migrant finding. In addition, breeding seabirds and farmland birds offer year round interest. Some of the more important sites are given below.

North of Stonehaven

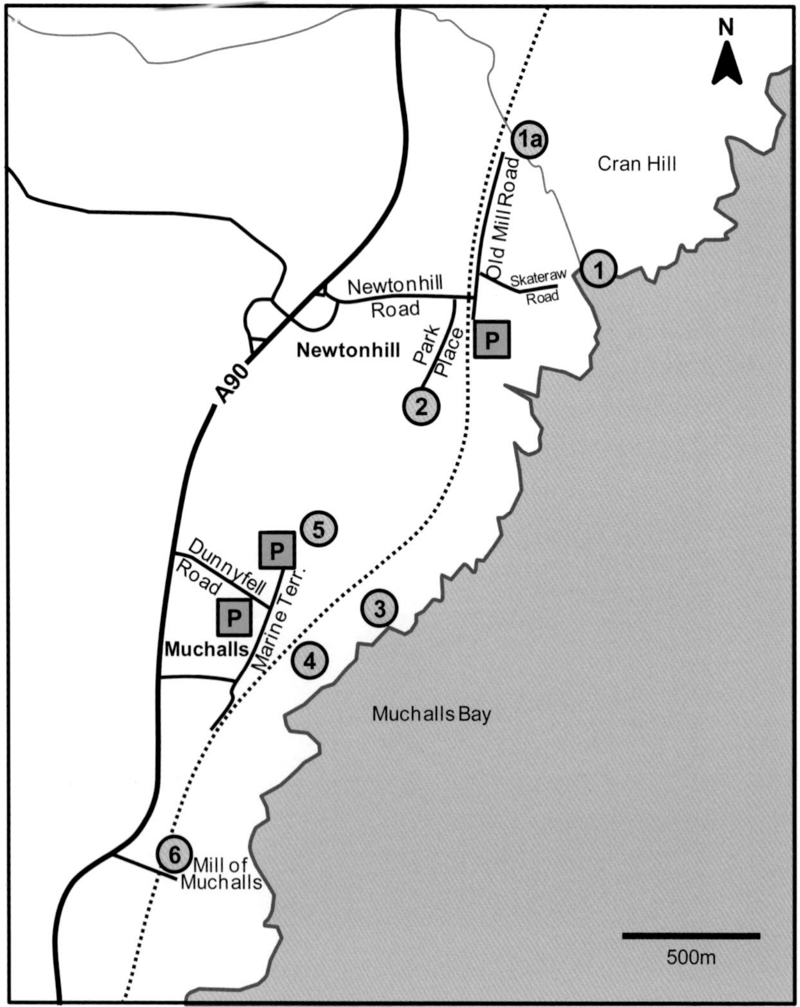

Newtonhill (NO 91 93)

Location & access: Situated between Portlethen and Stonehaven, Newtonhill can be accessed from the A90. There are plenty of parking spaces beside the Bettridge Centre (**NO 911 933**), reached by driving into the village and turning right after the railway bridge on Old Mill Rd.

Habitat and potential wildlife: The cliffs to the north and south of the small bay hold good numbers of nesting Fulmars, Kittiwakes and auks, including Puffins. Peregrines can be seen at almost any time of the year. The **Elsick Burn** (**1**) which runs into the bay is a home for nesting Dippers, Grey Wagtails, Reed Buntings and Sedge Warblers. In the autumn it has a good record for attracting migrants, with Pallas's or Yellow-browed Warblers seen almost annually in the trees around the **Elsick Mill** (**1a**) (**NO 912 939**).

The 'old village', east of the railway line, is always worth checking, particularly in late autumn. Its mature gardens, and also the shrubs beside the path down to the bay, have yielded a variety of migrants over the years. Booted Warbler, Icterine Warbler, Barred Warbler, Red-breasted Flycatcher and Nuthatch are among the rare species discovered here. The 'moor' is an area of gorse scrub on the path to Muchalls. It lies on the west side of the railway at the southern end of Park Place (**2**). In summer it holds nesting Linnets, Yellowhammers and Whitethroats, and in winter has produced Jack Snipe, Long-eared Owl and Woodcock. Sadly this area is zoned for possible housing development.

Yellowhammer *M. Sullivan*

Newtonhill has always proved to be a good sea-watching site. Up to 100 Bottlenose Dolphins have been seen on some August evenings, while White-beaked Dolphins and Minke Whales are also regular visitors. Large passages of Manx and Sooty Shearwaters have been recorded, along with the commoner skuas. It is worth noting that three of the first ten records of Cory's Shearwater in North-East Scotland came from Newtonhill, late July to early September being the best time for this species. Small numbers of Black Guillemots have bred around Muchalls Bay for at least 20 years (the southernmost breeding area on the British east coast), and can be seen from the cliffs south of Newtonhill. From the Bettridge Centre, walk south alongside the railway, past a football pitch, until you come to a stile. Once across, turn left and head towards the sea, keeping to the outside of the field. Then simply follow the coast (clambering over a low fence), until you reach an inlet just north of the Pheppie Burn (**NO 907 922**). The walk is about 2km each way.

Black Guillemots *M. Sullivan*

Muchalls (NO 90 92)

Location & access: Muchalls lies south of Newtonhill. Driving into Muchalls off the A90, turn right down Marine Terrace and park beside the village hall (**NO 902 919**), where there is room for about a dozen cars. If you wish to explore the Pheppie Burn, turn left into Monduff Road and park at the end of the track.

Habitat and potential wildlife: Check the trees around the village hall and the overgrown burn, then follow the track under a railway bridge towards the sea (**4**). The trees and bushes along this track can be full of birds given the right conditions. **Muchalls Bay**, with its impressive sea arches and stacks, is a lovely place to watch seabirds; gulls, auks, Fulmars, Eiders and Cormorants all nest here, and House Martins make their mud nests on the cliffs. Another spot worth a look is the **Pheppie Burn** (**5**) (**NO 904 925**) to the north of the village. This small burn flows through a patch of willows and gorse, and produced the region's first Marsh Warbler in 1993.

Easter Muchalls (**"Mill of Muchalls"**) (**6**), a small settlement some 600m to the south, contains a number of gardens with tall Sycamores, a duck pond, a stream and large areas of gorse and scrub attracting migrants in drift conditions. There are two possible routes on foot from Muchalls, both from the track leading to the sea described above. One follows the railway line south (turn right into the field immediately after the bridge) and the other runs along the top of the cliffs (turn right 100m further on). However, both tend to be very overgrown in summer. By car you can take a narrow track off the A90 at **NO 897 913** and park just under the viaduct by the mill pond. This track is signposted from the south, but not the north.

Small Pearl-bordered Fritillary *M. Sullivan*

There are several Northern Brown Argus colonies along the coast at Muchalls (check Rockrose areas) and a large colony of Small Pearl-bordered Fritillary at the base of Doonie Point between Muchalls and Easter Muchalls.

South of Stonehaven

The best sites lie adjacent to the A92, the coastal route south of Stonehaven.

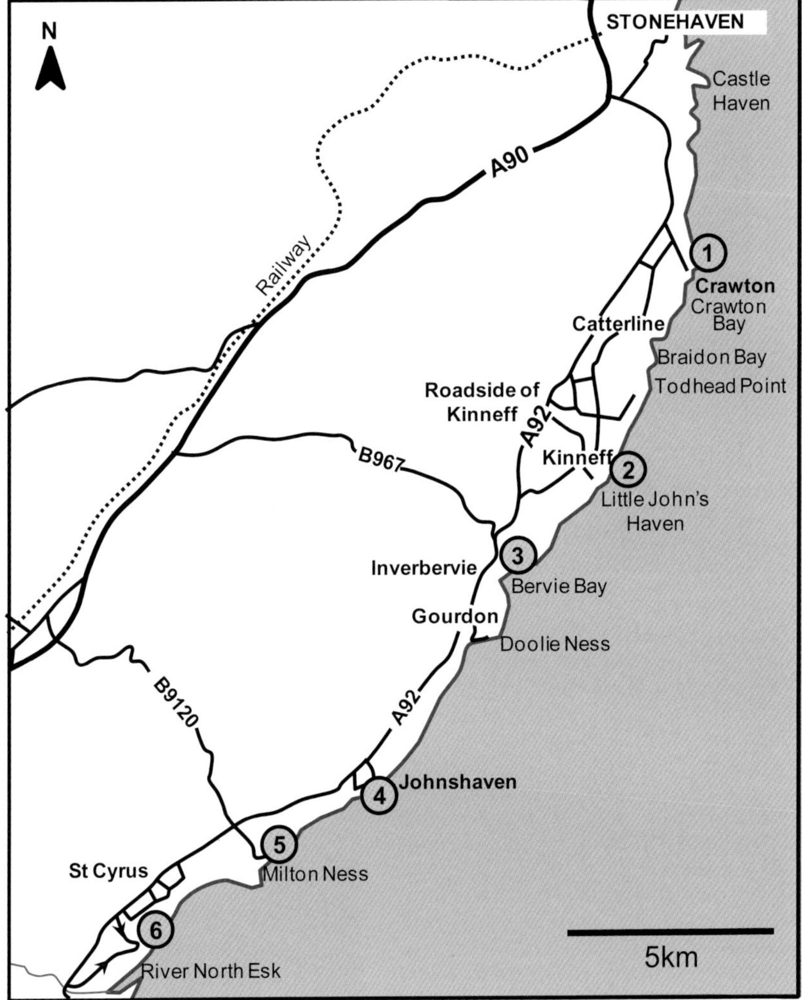

Fowlsheugh (NO 879 798)

Location & access: Fowlsheugh (**1**) is an RSPB reserve situated along the coast 4.8km south of Stonehaven. On the A92 heading south from Stonehaven, take the turning on the left signposted for Crawton. The reserve car park is on the right just before the end of this road. Parking spaces are limited. Please do not park at the reserve entrance or along the single-track road away from the car park.

Fowlsheugh *F. Sullivan*

Habitat and potential wildlife: Fowlsheugh is 2.5km of continuous spectacular cliffs with a narrow strip of cliff top grassland. The rock face has innumerable holes and ledges providing ideal nesting sites for seabirds. The site is one of the largest mainland seabird colonies in Britain and the main species (2012 populations) are Guillemot (44,700 individuals), Kittiwake (9439) and Razorbill (5195), with smaller numbers of Herring Gull, Fulmar, Puffin, Shag and Eider. The breeding season is from May-August and by the end of this period the cliffs can be very quiet, though it is always a splendid cliff-top walk. Aside from the seabirds, Peregrine is seen regularly, Raven has bred and farmland birds (including Whitethroat) breed. There is always potential for grounded migrants.

Fulmar *M. Sullivan*

Offshore, cetaceans can be seen, with regular Bottlenose Dolphin, while White-beaked Dolphin and Minke Whale can occur in July/August.

Kinneff (NO 856 748)

Location & access: 'Kinneff Old Church' (**2**) is located about 3.5km north-east of Inverbervie and is signposted off the A92. Heading south there is a turn-off to the left at the south end of Roadside of Kinneff. Follow the signs and park sensibly in the pull-off next to the church yard. Please respect the residents' privacy by staying to the road or track. Follow the road down the hill towards the sea, when it turns left round a building you continue along the unmade path towards the open fields. This path then bends right and follows a well vegetated gully eastwards to the sea.

Habitat and potential wildlife: This site, like many others, offers huge potential for finding migrant birds with its mature canopy of Sycamores, well-maintained gardens and scrubby bushes fringing the open fields.

Inverbervie (NO 834 725)

Location & access: This small coastal village (**3**) is approximately 15km south of Stonehaven on the A92. To reach the beach car park, take the turning opposite the village shop signposted 'beach' on Kirk Burn.

Habitat and potential wildlife: This whole area of coastline is very under-watched and would doubtless repay close attention. The best area to view the bay is from the public car park on the sea front. Many gulls bathe in the stream here and sea-duck and auks (which have included Black Guillemot) occur offshore in the bay. The coast north of the village is not easy to walk, but has a Cormorant colony and Peregrines can be seen. The wide, rocky seaweed-covered coast to the south is unusual for the north-east and similar to that just west of Fraserburgh. It extends several kilometres south to Johnshaven and holds numbers of waders, ducks and gulls. The gardens and trees in and around Inverbervie village are favourable for migrants (American Robin was recorded here in 1988) and of course the famous 'Bervie Chipper' comes heartily recommended!

Johnshaven (NO 795 671)

Location & access: Six kilometres south of Inverbervie lies the village of Johnshaven (**4**), accessed off the A92. In order to walk the coastal path north of the village, drive into the village centre via New Rd, continue past the Post Office and follow the road north past the harbour (Dock St, Fore Rd and Beach Rd.). After about 500m, a small parking area allows good views of the sea and the shoreline. The footpath continues northwards to Gourdon. Staying on Main St, heading south, and following West St. access to the coastline to the south of the village is possible. Follow the road until reaching the last line of houses. This footpath continues southwards to Miltonhaven (see below).

Habitat and potential wildlife: The many gardens in the village attract migrants during spring and autumn. The sea is worth a look, with Red-necked Grebe (check in the Eider flocks) and Black-throated Diver being found in the past. Seabird passage can be surprisingly productive here - the region's largest number of Black Terns (26) and Little Gulls (36) passed here in September 1997 and November 1998 respectively. The rocky shore extending north to Inverbervie provides suitable feeding areas for a variety of waders (including good numbers of Purple Sandpipers) and gulls.

One of the features of this part of the coastline is the impressive movement of passerines on visible migration during the autumn, particularly in September, when there is a light southwest wind. The first couple of hours after dawn can see hundreds of birds moving south, noticeably finches, pipits and hirundines, but often including wagtails (especially Grey), thrushes and buntings. Counts of 300+ Siskin an hour are not unusual. Slightly more unusual species caught up in the movement of commoner migrants include Snow and Lapland Bunting and Crossbill.

Miltonhaven (NO 774 656)

Location & access: Miltonhaven Caravan Park (**5**) can be accessed either by foot from Johnshaven (a brisk ten minute walk) or by car by following the signpost off the A92, 2km south of Johnshaven. When visiting this site by car, please park only at the car park of the caravan site – please do not park in access road lay-bys. The proprietors of the Caravan Park are only too pleased to have birders visiting the area and will often ask what's been seen.

Habitat and potential wildlife: This Sycamore-lined valley can be full of migrants given the right conditions. The line of Willows at the entrance to the Caravan Park can be particularly favoured by warblers. Walking north from the Caravan Park gives good views of the bay and Milton Ness, which holds a large concentration of gulls and terns in late summer. A beach here is one of the few such areas in this part of the region and, as such, can produce good numbers of Dunlin and Ringed Plover. A small pool in the field opposite the beach has produced freshwater species such as Curlew and Green Sandpiper.

St. Cyrus NNR (NO 742 634)

Location & access: St. Cyrus National Nature Reserve (**6**) occupies 92 hectares to the north of the River North Esk. The reserve is accessed off the A92 at two points. South of St. Cyrus village take the second road to the left, just after, and running down the side of, a mature strip of deciduous woodland. The road heads downhill to the reserve's visitor centre, car park and toilets. Heading north from Montrose on the A92, take the first small road to the right, signposted 'Beach', just after the River North Esk road-bridge.

Buzzard *M. Sullivan*

Habitat and potential wildlife: A wide variety of habitats is available. Mudflats and saltings dominate the estuary, and the long open beach with dunes backs onto large areas of open gorse scrub, willow herb and bushes. All of this is dominated to the west by high cliffs with bracken-covered lower slopes. The area is very good for moths, including specialities such as Bordered Grey; it is the best site in the region for Cinnabar Moth.

Small numbers of Fulmar breed on the cliffs along with a large, cliff-nesting House Martin colony at the northern limit of the reserve. Peregrine, Kestrel

St. Cyrus looking south to River North Esk *M. Sullivan*

and Buzzard also use the cliffs. North of the visitor centre is a large area of gorse scrub in which good numbers of breeding Stonechat, Whitethroat and Yellowhammer can be found along with a handful of Grasshopper Warblers. The northern end of the reserve has a rocky shore; in winter good numbers of Great Crested and occasional Slavonian Grebe can be seen from here. Birding from the beach and dunes can be frustrating due to the large number of dog walkers disturbing the birds, so it is recommended that an early visit is made, and if possible sunny weekends avoided.

The spit at the river-mouth provides an excellent roost for gulls and terns as they gather in their hundreds. Offshore in late summer has the spectacle of large rafts of sea-duck with up to 500 Common and Velvet Scoter and 550 Red-breasted Merganser. Kingfishers are often seen flying up and down the river accompanying Dipper, Grey Wagtail and Common Sandpiper.

5. INLAND TO THE CAIRNGORMS

North-East Scotland is not only justly famous for its coastal birding sites. Inland lies a wide range of habitats from lowland farms through to the high tops of the Cairngorms including ancient Scots Pine, Birch and Oak woodlands, pasture, lochs and heather moorland.

Lower Deeside – Aberdeen to Banchory

Loch of Skene / Garlogie Area (NJ 78 07)

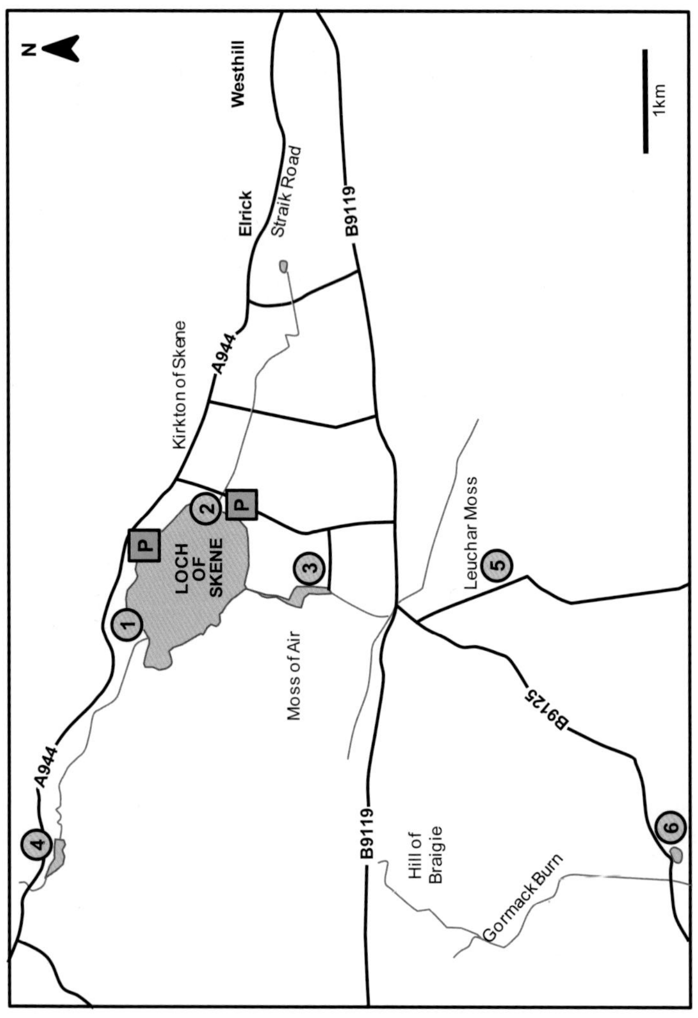

Location & access: Loch of Skene is a shallow freshwater loch on Dunecht Estate 13km west of Aberdeen on the A944. The north shore car park at **NJ 785 080** by the twin tower lodges is often used by those wishing to view the loch (please park away from the towers so as to not disturb the residents). It is possible to walk west along the marked track and find viewing points (**1**). There is also limited car parking in a small lay-by on the minor Garlogie road east of the loch. Follow a track through the trees to the east shore (**2**). There is no easy access to the south shore, and it is best to leave this area undisturbed.

Loch of Skene - looking west *J. Weston*

Habitat and potential wildlife: The loch is designated an SSSI, SPA and Ramsar wetland site, noted for its significant winter roosts of swans, geese, ducks, Coot and gulls. The loch covers 120ha, is generally no more than 2m deep, and fringed by reedbeds, small woodlands, a small heather moss and mixed agriculture fields. Several small man-made islands dot the loch. The loch is exposed and regularly partly freezes over in winter. Disturbance is generally low, with some fishing, and weekend sailing in spring and summer. Best viewing conditions are when overcast but clear, as bright sunlight reflecting off the water can make viewing from the north shore difficult.

The winter is the best time to visit when large numbers of over-wintering ducks and Coots, post-breeding Mute Swans, and large roosts of geese and gulls occur. Commonest duck species are Mallard, Tufted, Wigeon and Goldeneye, with a few Teal and Pochard. Goosanders roost on the loch overnight, but usually depart soon after dawn. Most of the North-East's rarer ducks have occurred on the loch in recent years and a careful check with a scope may reward a patient search. The winter goose roost can be spectacular. A pre-dawn visit gives great views of the thousands of mostly

Pink-footed Geese departing for the surrounding fields, but an evening visit can also be spectacular. The Greylag roost used to number up to 10,000, but is now only a few tens or hundreds of birds. Pink-feet numbers however have increased from a handful in the early 1990s to 15,000-30,000 (with a peak count of 48,000 in November 2014). A few Barnacles, and the occasional rarer White-fronted, Bean or even Snow Goose may occur. The winter gull roost builds from late afternoon as thousands of Common Gulls, and hundreds of Herring, Black-headed and Great Black-backed Gulls arrive from all directions. Fifteen to twenty thousand may be present on some days by dusk. The occasional white-winged gull may also be present.

In summer there is a reduction in activity on the loch. Other than wildfowl, Common Terns may hang around the loch and have bred. One or two pairs of Common Sandpipers regularly breed, and groups of Lapwing and Oystercatcher occur in spring. Occasional Greenshank, Redshank or Dunlin may visit in autumn, if water levels are low. Ospreys are regularly seen around and fishing on the loch, and Red Kites visit. The local small woodlands and fringing trees harbour the usual common passerines and raptors. Red squirrels also frequent the woods, and otter have been seen. Unfortunately mink are also known to occur.

Red Squirrel *M. Sullivan*

Other nearby sites

Driving the minor roads south of the Loch can produce farmland birds, including Red-legged Partridge, and there is a high chance of encountering Red Kites, along with Common Buzzards.

Garlogie Dam (**3**) (**NJ 784 061**): Site of the outfall stream from Loch of Skene, the dam and pond are approached down a rough unmarked track to the west of the minor Garlogie road, south of the A944. Mallard, Wigeon, Goldeneye, Coot and Moorhen are usual, plus one pair of breeding Mute Swans in spring and summer. Dipper and Grey Wagtail breed along the outfall burn.

Smew *M. Sullivan*

Waterton Loch (**4**) (**NJ 758 087**): A small loch to the south of the A944 just before entering the village of Dunecht. A few Mallard and Moorhen can be seen in the fringing reeds, plus the occasional Wigeon or Goldeneye on the loch. This is a site of a large spring gathering of Oystercatcher (>50) before they disperse further inland. Goosander and Smew have occurred.

Red Kite *P. Newman*

Cullerlie Standing Stones / Leuchar Moss (5) (NJ 785 042): South of the B9119 and B9125 junction at Garlogie, a minor road heads south-east to the stone circle. Parking here gives a view over Leuchar Moss to the north. This is a good place to see Red Kites and Buzzards. Thrushes and finches feed on the fields, and Lapwings gather in good numbers.

Roadside pools at Cullerlie (6) (NJ 758 027): There are several pools and low-lying wet fields in the vicinity of Cullerlie. The main one lies by the side of the B9125 at the grid reference above - there is a small car park next to it, on the bend. Another, just to the north can be viewed from the minor road at **NJ 764 035**. Others are visible from these roads and their extent depends on groundwater levels. These ponds are always worth checking. They hold small numbers of ducks (Mallard, Teal, Wigeon and Shoveler) and breeding and passage waders, along with gulls. Sometimes the birds are close, offering good views.

Loch of Leys (1) (NO 710 975)

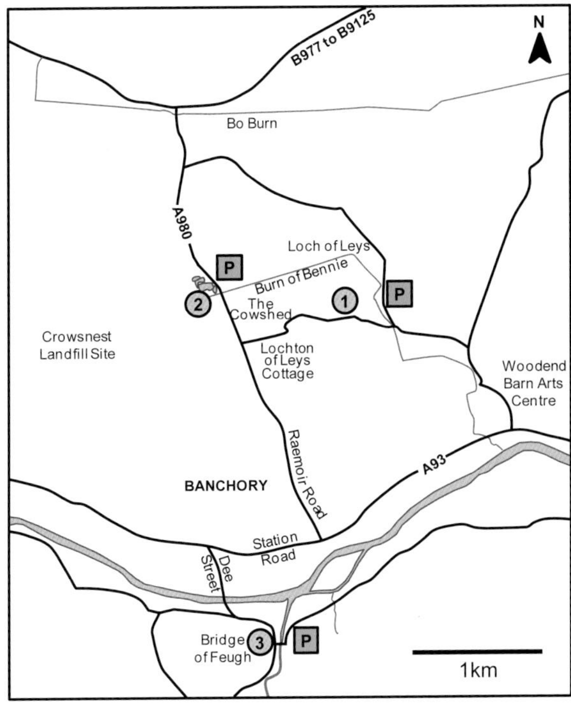

Location & access: Lying just north of Banchory, it is possible to walk out and back along the southern side from a small roadside car park at the grid reference above. To the west lies the Raemoir Fishery (**2**). It is possible, with permission, to park here, and the staff members are interested in bird sightings.

Loch of Leys *I. Francis*

Habitat and potential wildlife: This former loch is now an extensive fen and swamp, containing an old crannog. Open water is now almost non-existent, but the sedge and reedbeds with scrub hold many Sedge Warblers and Reed Buntings, with Grasshopper Warblers often present. Water Rails can be found across the site – always heard but rarely seen. Mallard, Teal and Snipe breed, with Curlew and Lapwing nearby. There is a good range of common songbirds and Tawny and Long-eared Owls can be heard here, with displaying ("roding") Woodcock a common sight in May and June. The reedbeds at the western end by the fishery can hold a swallow roost and Starlings also roost here. The fishery has held a wintering Great Grey Shrike, and Ospreys can be seen in summer.

Common Snipe *R. Humphreys*

Bridge of Feugh (3) (NO 701 950)

Just south of Banchory lies the Bridge of Feugh. A car park is available east of the bridge. Salmon can be watched leaping the falls in spring as they run upstream to breed. Dipper and Grey Wagtail can be found feeding in the falls.

Forest of Birse

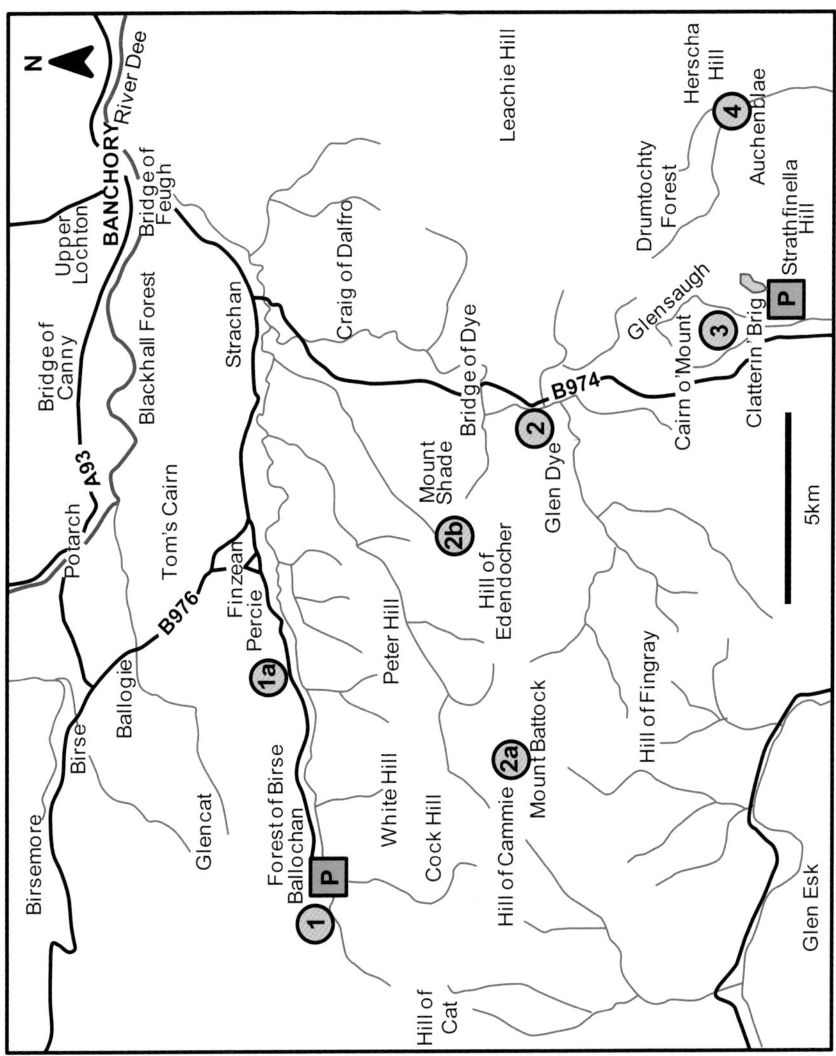

Location & access: The Forest of Birse (**1**) (**NO 53 90**) is an area of highland forming the catchment of the River Feugh. It lies west of the village of Finzean (excellent food at Finzean Farm teashop (NO 604 929)). From Banchory follow the B974 west along the River Feugh, merging onto the B976 at Strachan. Follow signs for Forest of Birse, passing a signed turn-off for the

Finzean Farm tea room. The single track road passes through an area of riparian woodland (with a woodland walk along the river), before coming out into a large area of open moorland, with pine plantation and scattered regenerating Scots Pine. Park in the area indicated at the head of the road before reaching the farms. A series of paths lead west and north from this car park. It is suggested that the path westwards (Aboyne and Glen Esk) be followed.

Forest of Birse *P. Grant*

Habitat and potential wildlife: The footpath passes through an area of improved pasture, with open fields. Above the farmland a large area of heather moor covers the low hills. Walking is easy, and generally level. Spring and summer visits can turn up the regular upland species, Dipper and Grey Wagtail along the river, Redstart and Spotted Flycatcher in the riparian woodland (try around the old chapel by the car park) and Ring Ouzel in the higher moors. Released Red-legged Partridge can be seen anywhere along the road. On the heather moor, Red Grouse can be common, and Black Grouse are present. Keep an eye out for raptors, the commonest being Buzzard, but Red Kite, Peregrine, Merlin, Golden Eagle and even White-tailed Eagle could occur. This area used to be very good for Hen Harriers, but nowadays they are rare, though still possible. Although the area can be bleak in winter, a walk on a clear cold still day can be exhilarating with large flocks of finches feeding in cover crops, raptors and ravens overhead, and the calls of Red Grouse heard over the sound of the river.

Red Grouse *P. Newman*

Returning towards **Woodend** (**1a**) (about 5km east) watch the power lines and tree tops in winter for occasional Great Grey Shrike or Stonechat in summer. Pull into an old quarry on the left and park, then follow the marked woodland path crossing the river. Tits and finches form flocks in winter, while warblers (Willow and Chiffchaff, with Blackcap) can be seen and heard in summer. Dipper and Grey Wagtail nest along the stream.

Great Grey Shrike *M. Sullivan*

Glen Dye (2) (NO 64 84)

Location & access: Some 15km south of Banchory on the B974, the best access point is from a small roadside car park where the road crosses the Water of Dye (**NO 651 860**). Several linear or circular walks of varying difficulty can be made from here.

Upper Glen Dye *P. Grant*

Habitat and potential wildlife: This large upland glen offers a chance to see the typical range of north-east woodland and moorland birds. To the north and east, there are extensive plantation woodlands of mixed species and ages. These can yield a wide range of woodland species, including crossbills, Sparrowhawk, Goshawk, Buzzard, Woodcock, Tree Pipit, Spotted Flycatcher, Siskin and sometimes Long-eared Owl. West of the road, and out to the blanket bogs of Mount Battock

Black Grouse *P. Newman*

(**2a**), the range of possible species within the glen (mostly in summer) includes Teal, Black Grouse, Red Grouse, Hen Harrier (now very rare), Merlin, Peregrine, Curlew, Snipe, Short-eared Owl, Cuckoo, Dipper, Grey Wagtail, Wheatear and Stonechat. The higher tops have Golden Plovers. Adders are abundant in summer, and can be found basking on the paths. **Clachnaben** (**2b**) (**NO 614 865**) is a spectacular granite tor with a fine view, and well worth the ascent. Large Heath butterflies have recently been found in Glen Dye and Water Voles are present.

Glensaugh (3) (NO 668 788)

Location & access: Glensaugh can be reached by parking at the Glensaugh Research Station (James Hutton Institute) and walking down the minor road toward Clatterin' Brig. Take the track on the right to reach the lower part of the glen and walk north up the glen along the Slack Burn. Self-guided trail leaflets are available at the research station.

Habitat and potential wildlife: Glensaugh is a narrow, flat-bottomed valley extending for 3-5km into the eastern Cairngorms. The lower valley slopes are wooded, and the valley bottom is used for sheep and cattle grazing. The upper valley slopes reach up to open moorland. In the summer, the valley is home to typical upland breeding birds, including Wheatear, Whinchat and Stonechat, with Peregrine, Red and Black Grouse present at higher altitudes. Cuckoos search for Meadow Pipit nests. Grey Wagtail frequents the Slack Burn. Loch Saugh can hold small numbers of ducks and Mute Swan. Dark Green and Pearl-bordered Fritillaries are present and Common Lizards can be seen.

Grey Wagtail *R. Humphreys*

Auchenblae (4) (NO 727 786)

Location & access: Continue east along the minor road from Glensaugh to Auchenblae. The community-owned park, known as the Den, is situated on the western outskirts of the village and can be reached from the village square.

Habitat and potential wildlife: the village itself is used for nesting by House Martins and Swallows. Swifts are also present, but have decreased in number in recent years. The Den provides a wooded and shrub habitat and also a small stream which is used by breeding Dippers. The shrubs and trees which cover the valley sides are home to a wide variety of breeding birds in the summer, including Willow and Sedge Warblers, Spotted Flycatcher, Blackcap, Whitethroat, Lesser Redpoll, Tree Sparrow and Tawny Owl. Sparrowhawks and Buzzards are also to be seen.

Sedge Warbler *F. Sullivan*

Mid-Deeside Aboyne to Ballater Area

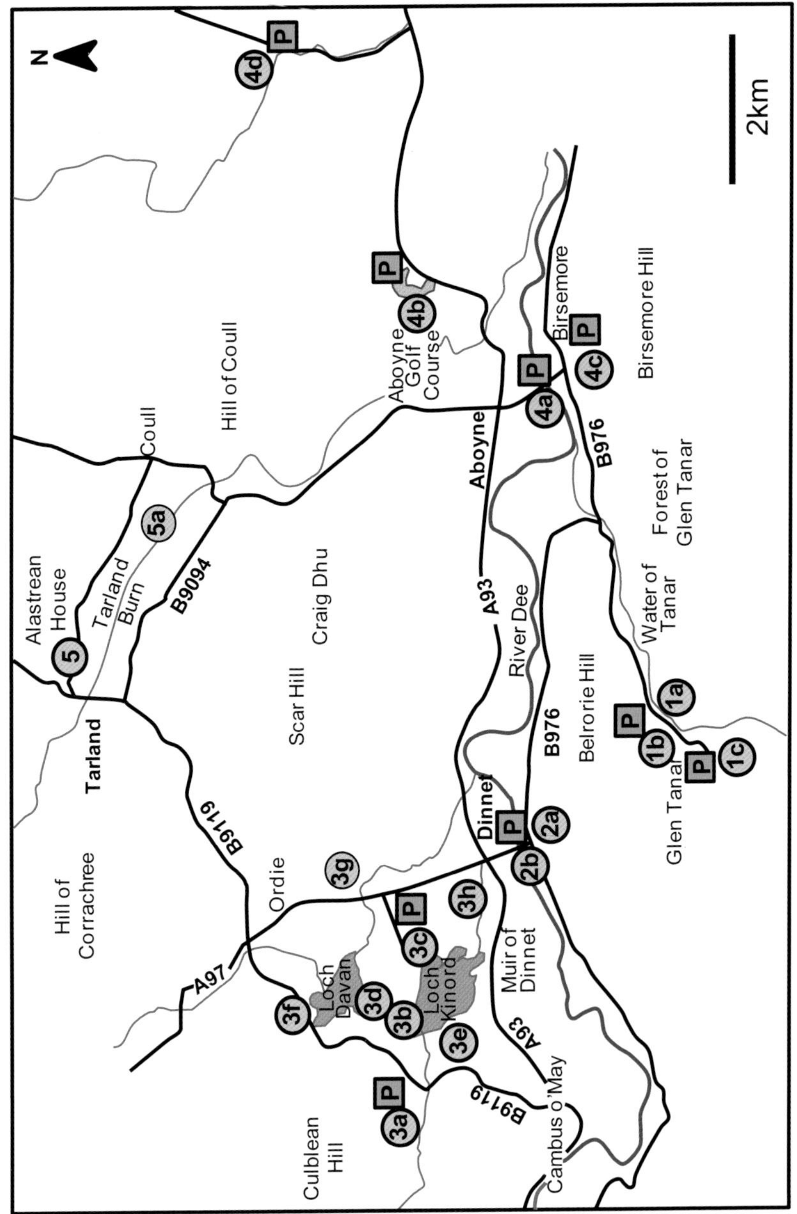

Glen Tanar (1) (NO 48 95)

Glen Tanar Estate is a National Nature Reserve and one of the best highland estates managed for pastoral farming, amenity and wildlife, as well as country sports. It supports a range of habitats in a series of valleys, from riparian woodland, birch wood, grazed valley floors, pine and larch plantations and ancient Caledonian Pine forest, topped by heather moor and high pastures. It stretches from the Dee Valley to the peaks of the southern Grampians at Mount Keen (939m). The Glen is best visited during the breeding season from March until July, although resident raptors and grouse can be seen all year and winter flocks of thrushes and foraging forest passerines show well on bright winter days. Some of the most productive walks and sites are described below.

Glen Tanar Pinewoods *I. Francis*

Location & access: The Glen is located off the B967 South Deeside Road, 3km west of the Aboyne Bridge. If approaching from the east (Aboyne), turn left up the "C" road into the Glen at Brig o'Ess and the Tower House at NO 505 973. Park after 3km at **NO 479 965** Braeloine car park (small charge), where there is a visitor centre and toilets, or at the road end car park near the estate offices at **NO 474 956**. Most of the sites and walks are accessible from one of these two locations. Some of the best walking circuits are as follows:

Chapel and Loch circuit (1a) (3.5km)

From Braeloine, cross the river and walk up stream or across the fields past the chapel on marked paths. Then head upstream to Knockie Bridge. From here continue up the track for access to upper Glen Tanar and the Caledonian Pine forests or cross the bridge and follow the path around Glen Tanar Loch and back via the estate buildings and along the road to Braeloine. This route can be extended along the Queen's Drive (below), back to Braeloine (extra 1km).

Habitat and potential wildlife: The woodland at Braeloine and the adjacent Water of Tanar, seen from the old pack horse bridge, can produce breeding Tree Pipit, Redstart, Spotted Flycatcher and on the river, Dipper, Common Sandpiper and Grey Wagtail, as well as more common breeders and Red Squirrel, all with little walking. This route continues through valley bottom farmland towards the mixed riparian and pine woodlands upstream. This route is accessible all year.

Queen's Drive circuit (1b) (3.5km)

From the road end car park at the estate offices follow the way-marked track uphill past the buildings and turn right (north) onto the Queen's Drive at the top. The track contours round above the valley bottom and joins the Firmouth Road after 2km, at NO 477 968. Follow this road down a short way to a pedestrian gate on the right. Follow the wide path down through the field and Juniper grove to Braeloine car park and return to the road end car park along the road. This route can be extended via the river route from Braeloine, described above, back to the road end car park (4.5km). There is no public bridge before Knockie Bridge.

Habitat and potential wildlife: Both the above routes pass through the fields and woodland of lower Glen Tanar and are the best areas in spring for breeding passerines described above, passage waders on the fields and farmland birds such as Yellowhammer, Whitethroat and Redpoll. Mandarin Duck has occurred on the river near the house. In winter, feeding flocks of Fieldfare, Redwing and Mistle Thrush are often present unless there is snow cover. Both Greater Spotted and Green Woodpeckers are often heard and sometimes are visible, especially in the birch wood off the Queen's Road. Cuckoo is regular and Bullfinch occurs in the young trees near the saw mill. The route gives open views over the valley, so look overhead for soaring Golden Eagle, Osprey, Goshawk, Sparrowhawk, Peregrine and Buzzard. Ospreys may fish on the Loch, which can be otherwise rather unproductive, save for the odd Heron and Grey Wagtail.

Water of Tanar at Etnach, above the forest *P. Grant*

Upper Glen Tanar (1c) (8–20km)

Start at the road end car park. There are numerous circuits; please stick to established paths during the breeding season. Expect to walk an 8-10km round trip to get to the best Caledonian Pine forest in mid-Glen Tanar, the Drum and Glen Allachy and an 18km round trip to get to Etnach, Shiel of Glen Tanar and upper Glen Allachy. These places are the jewels of mid and upper Glen Tanar and well worth the walk or cycle. Alternatively, the estate does guided Landrover trips, saving a long walk and offers photographic visits to a Golden Eagle hide and other specialist hides, covering a range of other raptors and song birds, for a fee (www.glentanar.co.uk/activities).

Habitat and potential wildlife: Forest birds such as all three crossbills, Redstart, Tree Pipit, Goldcrest, Great Spotted Woodpecker, Treecreeper and Siskin are found. Scottish and Common Crossbills can occur in large foraging flocks in winter, whilst Parrot Crossbills prefer the upper forest, along the tree line. Whitethroat, Stonechat, Whinchat and Willow Warbler have notable populations in the open heath areas amongst the forest. Goshawk is present, along with Tawny Owl. Capercaillie is still present but is now very rare. Please do not disturb during the lekking season in March/April or through the breeding season – and please stay on the tracks. Forest edge areas can be good for Green Hairstreaks.

"Pine" Crossbill sp. *P. Newman*

Higher up, the heather moor is alive with Meadow Pipits and Skylark and there is a good population of attendant Cuckoos. The estate is managed for low intensity Red Grouse shooting. Black Grouse can be seen lekking at Etnach well into the summer, along with breeding Curlew, Redshank, Lapwing, Snipe, Oystercatcher, Northern Wheatear and Short-eared Owl. There are Goosander and Common Sandpiper on the river and higher up, at Shiel of Glen Tanar, the old grazings attract foraging Ring Ouzel from breeding sites on the screes above. Merlin may be seen.

Black Grouse *P. Newman*

Hen Harrier *R. Humphreys*

Golden Plover and Ptarmigan can be found on the upper slopes of Mount Keen; follow the mountain path across the foot-bridge.

Golden Eagles are present on the estate and can be seen at times over the woodlands and hills. Ospreys also nest nearby and may pass to fish at the Dinnet lochs. Hen Harriers are encouraged at Glen Tanar and occasionally breed, but they are rare here due to persecution on other east Grampian moors. Watch for them hunting over the moor.

Dinnet Oakwood and Bridge (2) (NO 462 983)

Location & access: Dinnet Oakwood (**2a**) is a National Nature Reserve located off the B976 South Deeside Road, immediately opposite the south end of Dinnet Bridge. Park at the north side of the bridge and walk over. Please do not park in the fisherman's lay-by on the south side. Spend time watching the river both upstream and downstream off the bridge (**2b**) as it regularly produces good close views of Dipper, Common Sandpiper, Grey Wagtail and a nice range of breeding birds in the surrounding trees. Access to the wood is via a pedestrian gate on to a path that is part of the Core Path network, giving a good route over to Glen Tanar. Work the wood from this path.

Habitat and potential wildlife: The wood is primarily Oak, Ash and Birch with some mature Scots Pine and other conifers. It has been a site for Wood Warbler but this species has been absent in recent years. Redstart, Spotted Flycatcher and more common breeding passerines can be found, along with a good population of Great Spotted Woodpecker and the occasional Green Woodpecker. Tawny Owl, Red Kite, Goshawk and Woodcock have all been seen. The wood is best visited in the breeding season.

Muir of Dinnet National Nature Reserve (NO 44 99)

http://www.nnr-scotland.org.uk/muir-of-dinnet/

Muir of Dinnet is a beautiful highland NNR extending to 1163ha. It is managed by Scottish Natural Heritage and covers an extensive area of upland and lowland heath, pine and birch wood, old pasture, lochs and wetland. It therefore provides a range of habitats, many marked walking routes and wildlife interest all year. The reserve is also known for moths, butterflies, damselflies and Otter. The Kentish Glory moth has its stronghold here, needing self-seeded, young (head-high) birch such as that at **NO 433 981**. The flight period for this moth is late April to mid-May.

Location & access: The Reserve Centre is at **Burn o'Vat** (**3a**) (**NO 429 997**) on the B9119. From Dinnet (NO 459 987) travel 3.5km west on the A93 and turn right onto the B9119. The Visitor Centre, toilets and free parking are on the left, 2.5km from the junction. There are many walking routes from this point and information and the warden are located here. All routes offer varied habitat with good birding opportunities. Some of the best are listed below.

Burn o'Vat circuit (**4km**)**:** This route follows paths up towards Culblean Hill to the west of the Burn o'Vat Centre; from the centre car park walk past the toilets towards the Vat. The Vat is an impressive cave-like pothole gouged out by glacial melt-water about 14,000 years ago. Return towards the car park and follow the path uphill for an overview of the woodland and Loch Kinord. Scan for raptors. After 1km, the path joins the old Culblean track where extensive views of the reserve are obtained. Turn right and follow the track north to the junction with the B9119. Cross over and then follow the path close to the road, back through woodland to the Burn o'Vat car park.

Tree Pipit *M. Sullivan*

Habitat and potential wildlife: The immediate vicinity of the car park and centre is in open woodland and often holds Blackcap and Garden Warbler and has breeding Spotted Flycatcher. Both Pied Flycatcher and Wood Warbler have sung here in recent years but have not bred. On the hillside the path passes through mixed plantation forest to the tree line. Above the tree line is dry montane heath and heather. Look out for raptors, Common Crossbill, Meadow and Tree Pipit, Redstart, Skylark, Stonechat and Cuckoo. Adders can be found on warm early spring days, and both Pearl-bordered and Small Pearl-bordered Fritillaries can be found in summer. Just north of the junction of the Culblean track and the B9119 (at around **NJ 434 011**), a set of small overgrown pools holds Northern Damselfly.

Loch Kinord circuit (**3b**) (**5km**): Starting at the Burn o'Vat Centre, cross the road and follow the marked path east to Old Kinord. Turn south towards the ancient Pictish cross and New Kinord. A small path follows the northern edge of Loch Kinord and then turns back "inland" towards New Kinord Farm. (It is possible to park here at **NJ 452 002** - access from the A97 at NJ 455 003 (**3c**)). Continue the circuit, by turning north on a path towards Loch Davan and the ancient hut circles. Then turn west along the established track back to Old Kinord and Burn o'Vat. Access to Loch Davan (**3d**) can be obtained via a small path towards the loch, just west of the pedestrian pass gate and wall found on the track from the hut circles that heads towards Old Kinord.

Habitat and potential wildlife: The route gives access to the loch margins and passes through old pasture and mixed pine and birch woodland. In the summer, breeding Goldeneye and other waterfowl can be seen in the bays and reeds. The area is particularly good for woodpeckers, Redstart and Tree Pipit. Spotted Flycatcher breeds at New Kinord and many common warblers, particularly Willow Warbler also breed here. In the winter the route gives good vantage points across the lochs, and occasionally wintering Great Grey Shrike can be found. It is good for foraging flocks of tits, Treecreeper and Redpoll. In summer, Adders and Common Lizards can be seen, along with Scotch Argus butterflies.

Lesser Redpoll *P. Newman*

Parkin's Moss Trail (**3e**) (**3km**)**:** From the Burn o'Vat Centre follow the dragonfly marked trail through woodland, heather and raised bog.

Habitat and potential wildlife: This route is excellent for butterflies, day-flying moths and dragonflies. It is best to do this on a warm summer's day. Keep a look out for Adders and Roe Deer.

Loch Davan viewpoint (**3f**)**:** Loch Davan is the less disturbed of the two main lochs due to its limited accessibility. It is therefore often more productive for birds, particularly waterfowl. A lay-by on the B9119 just West of Glen Davan House at **NJ 438 012** provides a view across the loch, from the road (though a telescope is very useful). Please avoid disturbance on foot around this loch as much as possible.

Loch Davan from Culblean Hill *I. Francis*

Habitat and potential wildlife: Reeds and open water attract wildfowl, including Whooper Swans in winter. In recent years Ring-necked Ducks have arrived on spring passage in March / April. In very cold weather the loch can partially or completely freeze over. In spring and summer large concentrations of hirundines can occur, and otter might be seen through the year.

Other adjacent sites

Ordie Moss (**3g**)**:** for wetland birds such as breeding Snipe, Redshank, Curlew, Grasshopper Warbler and Reed Bunting. Willow Warbler is common. Great Grey Shrike can hunt here in winter. Park at Ordie Crossroads (1.25km East of Loch Davan, at **NJ 449 020**) and walk east along the public road to Tarland or south on the A97.

Clarack Loch, Dinnet: This spot is 1km north of the Dinnet Oakwood just by Dinnet Village on the A93 and the two make an interesting combined visit. The Clarack Loch path is multi-purpose and wheelchair accessible. Walk north from the Dinnet car park at **NO 459 987** onto the path that heads north-east behind the Loch Kinord Hotel. Continue towards Clarack Loch where a timber deck built over the loch gives excellent views. Return by the same route or continue on a rougher path to Loch Kinord. The route passes through old birch and pine woodland. The Clarack Loch is a small, reed-encircled stretch of water backed by trees. The route is best in the breeding season but is also quite good for wintering water birds. One or two pairs of Goldeneye and Mute Swans nest on the loch and Grey Heron is regular. The woodland carries many of the birds characteristic of the Muir of Dinnet. The village car park area and the scrub woodland behind is worth checking for tit flocks, and breeding Long-tailed Tit, Spotted Flycatcher, Greenfinch and Chiffchaff.

Goldeneye *M. Sullivan*

Aboyne (4) (NO 52 98)

Location & access: The north bank of the Dee from Aboyne Bridge (NO 524 979) downstream is conveniently accessible via a footpath through the riverside woodland and heath. Currently there is no circular route, so after a kilometre or so it is necessary to return along the same path. To access the river, park on Charlestown Road in the vicinity of the Boat Inn. Toilets and services are available here or in the village.

Habitat and potential wildlife: The route is best visited in the spring and early summer, during the breeding season, when it can be highly productive for breeding woodland, farmland and river birds. It can be inaccessible if water levels are high or when growth obscures the path in late summer. The habitat is typical riverine woodland, pasture and heath. Extensive views of the river can be obtained from the bridge or the path. The river bank close to the Boat Inn holds a Garden Warbler territory and nearby large gardens and woodland can produce Siskin, Goldcrest, Bullfinch and Spotted Flycatcher. Watch the river for Dipper, Goosander and Heron and check Mallard flocks for the occasional more unusual duck. Oystercatcher and Common Sandpiper breed on both banks and Curlew pass through. Look out for at least one pair of breeding Redshank. Common Terns and Black-headed Gulls favour a shingle bar on the opposite bank, about 1km downstream of the bridge. When suitable river bank conditions are available, Sand Martin colonies can develop. Look out for regular Common Buzzard, as they breed just upstream. Ospreys sometimes fish this stretch of the river. The trees along the

Oystercatcher *P. Newman*

Sand Martins *M. Sullivan*

fence line and the bank-side gorse are particularly productive for Linnet, Yellowhammer, Meadow Pipit, Dunnock and Wren. Song Thrush, Redpoll and Whitethroat are also possible. Check the wet flashes in the arable fields to the north side for Curlew, Oystercatcher, Heron and Lapwing. Otters are present on the river here, and the 5-spot Ladybird has been recorded.

Also in the area

Aboyne Loch (**4b**) has wintering and breeding duck including Tufted, Goosander, occasional Merganser and Goldeneye. Sedge Warbler, Reed Bunting, Kingfisher, Water Rail, Mute Swan, and feeding Osprey are regular in summer. Circumnavigate on foot via an established route (keep to loch edge and watch for stray golf balls), park in the lay-by on A93 (**NO 540 998**). Pearl-bordered Fritillaries are present north of the loch.

Aboyne Loch *I. Francis*

Birsemore Loch (**4c**) (lying south of the river) for breeding Little Grebe, Coot and visiting Heron and Kingfisher. Circumnavigate on foot, park in the lay-by on the C class road to Mains of Balfour (**NO 528 974**).

Auchlossan (**4d**) lies 2km north on the C class road from the A93 at Dess, between Aboyne and Kincardine O'Neil. Best in winter for Pink-footed Geese, ducks and Common Gulls and during spring and late summer/autumn for passage waders and Wagtails (Pied and White, also at Aboyne Green), particularly when the fields are flooded. This area holds good numbers of breeding farmland waders. Observe from the bank opposite Deeside Activities Centre and facilities; there is no easy access to the site. Park at the Centre (**NJ 567 015**) where there is a café, shop and WC.

Auchlossan Floods *I. Francis*

Tarland Waste Water Treatment Works and Woodland (5)

Location & access: The Scottish Water Waste Water Treatment Works (WWTW) settlement ponds take treated water from the works, and maintain an important local breeding and roosting place for wildfowl, waders and geese. The open pools are gradually vegetating over, and water levels can vary, reducing their attractiveness to waterfowl. A hide and small car park (**NJ 487 043**) lie on the C class Tarland to Coull road, running east from Tarland. A circular walk from Tarland taking in the hide and continuing east, then around the golf course and Alastrean House policies (2.5km) passes through a variety of habitat.

Habitat and potential wildlife: The WWTW ponds and surrounding fields, particularly those to the east are of interest all year round. In winter there are several hundred (sometimes thousands) of grazing Pink-footed Geese on the fields and Mallard and Wigeon on the ponds. Spring brings an influx of waders. Several hundred Golden Plover, Lapwing, Curlew, Oystercatcher and a few Redshank and Snipe pass through, whilst

Curlew *R. Humphreys*

there is a breeding population of Curlew, Oystercatcher, Lapwing and Redshank. Red-necked Phalarope and Black-tailed Godwit have been recorded here. Pied Wagtail, Bullfinch, Yellowhammer and Meadow Pipit breed in the vicinity, as well as Siskin, Goldcrest, Goldfinch and Buzzard in the pine wood behind. The woodland on the Alastrean Estate is good for a range of species including Tawny Owl, Spotted Flycatcher and Mistle Thrush.

Also in the area

Coull fields and floods (**5a**) (**NJ 511 026**) for wintering duck and geese and passage waders including large numbers of Lapwing. The low ground along the Tarland Burn floods and can produce extensive pools in wet periods. Observe from the Tarland to Coull road (C class public road) at small lay-bys between the Tarland WWTW and the bridge at NJ 510 025. The open water can render these fields more productive than the Tarland WWTW ponds.

Coull Floods *I. Francis*

Around Ballater

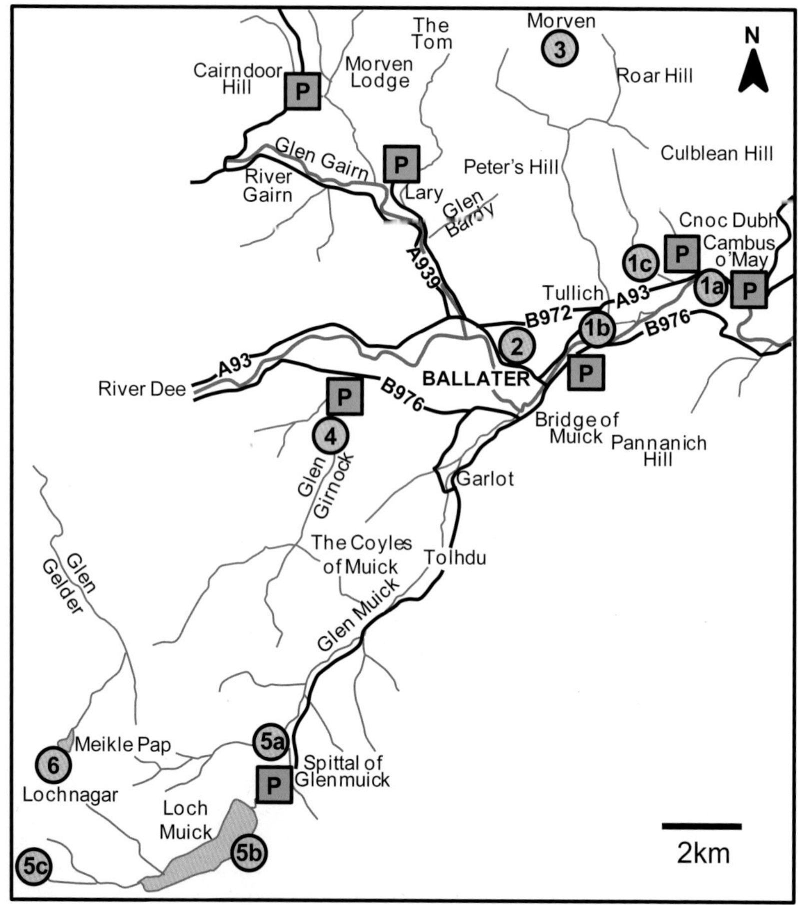

Cambus o'May to Ballater via Pannanich (south of the River Dee)

Location & access: Cambus o'May footbridge crosses the River Dee from a point on the A93, on the north side of the river, between Ballater to the west and the B9119 turn to Tarland to the east. The walking route is part of the newly developed Core Paths system in the area (**1a**). Park at the car park at Cambus o'May (**NO 423 975)**, and descend to the old Deeside railway line and the river. Cross the bridge to the south bank. Follow the way-marked path into the woodland, turning west at the plantation track. Continue through to Pannanich.

An alternative approach is to park at the Pannanich Forest lay-by on the B976 at **NO 381 963**. Walk east along the road for about 200m to a gate and way marker, leading into a track that descends towards the river (**1b**). The route continues to Cambus o'May (3.75km). A longer route, crossing the river at Ballater Bridge and taking in the Deeside railway path completes a circular (12km) route from Cambus o'May. The Deeside railway path gives good views over agricultural fields, and in autumn is good for mixed foraging flocks of finches and tits. The **Tulloch Fishery** (**1c**) (**NO 395 977**) north of the river is visible from the track or can be visited separately by car. In the breeding season, it is worth checking for fishing Osprey in the early evening. It has a population of Mallard but produces few other waterfowl.

Habitat and potential wildlife: South from Cambus o'May, and across the suspension bridge, the path runs through open Pine, Oak, Juniper and Birch woodland then a further pine plantation with old Birch, Larch and Pine, leading to the river bank. There is a beautiful section through small meadows at Pannanich, where a good population of Spotted Flycatcher persists. The mixed habitat produces a range of woodland, river and meadow species, including Great Spotted and the occasional Green Woodpeckers, Tree Pipit, Willow and Garden Warbler, Blackcap, Redstart, Siskin, Goldcrest, Woodcock and Buzzard. There are good views of the river with its stony shingle bars and riverine meadows. Look out for nesting waders such as Common Sandpiper, Oystercatcher and Ringed Plover. Common, Herring and Black-headed Gulls frequently use the river. Towards the north end of the walk, at NO 386 965, just downstream of the Pannanich fishing hut, there are excellent views of the hills to the north, around Tullich and the Crannoch. This a good spot for a late afternoon raptor watch. Osprey, Buzzard, Sparrowhawk, Kestrel, Goshawk and Golden Eagle are all possible. Look across the river to a large area of dry gorse scrub for Yellowhammer, Linnet and Whitethroat, with Grey and Pied Wagtails along the river banks. Hirundines, including Sand Martin feed over the area. In spring there are ducks and occasional passage waders such as Curlew, Redshank and Lapwing in the vicinity of the fields around the old Ballater waste water treatment works pond, on the north bank.

Osprey *R. Humphreys*

Craigendarroch Oakwood (NO 365 965)

Location & access: Craigendarroch (**2**) lies between the A93 and the Pass of Ballater (the B972). Park in Ballater, and follow the A93 west to the paths through the wood. There are several access points to this very prominent, steep wooded craggy hill which overlooks the village. Paths wind uphill to the top, where there

Craigendarroch Oakwood *I. Francis*

is an excellent view over the densely wooded landscape of Deeside to the mountains beyond.

Habitat and potential wildlife: The oak woodland is a Site of Special Scientific Interest. The oaks peter out up the hill to be succeeded by pine and birch-dominated woodland, which in turn gives way to rocks and moorland. The range of birds in the wood is not very wide, but includes Redstart, Stock Dove and Spotted Flycatcher, and in some years Wood Warbler. This used to be a reliable site for them, but they have become rarer. There are also Green and Great Spotted Woodpeckers in the area. Buzzard nest in the woods and there are good views of breeding Jackdaw.

Wood Warbler *M. Sullivan*

Morven (NJ 377 040)

Morven from Lary *P. Grant*

Location & access: This 871m high hill (**3**) offers commanding views over Deeside and is relatively easily ascended, though the climb is inevitably quite steep. There are several potential access points. To the west, it is possible to park by the A939 around **NJ 312 027** and walk in via Morven Lodge, or walk from the Lary road (**NO 338 997**). Please park sensibly. From the south, access can be gained from the Forestry Commission car park at **NO 403 981**, off the A93 via the Crannach. From the east, it is possible to walk in from Tillypronie at **NJ 422 076** or from the Groddie road at **NJ 410 048** (again, please park sensibly). In all cases, expect to walk an 8-12km round trip with considerable ascent.

Habitat and potential wildlife: The top of Morven holds small numbers of Ptarmigan, which can be seen more easily in autumn and winter. Mountain Hares can be quite confiding here. The area around the hill consists of base-rich grassland with extensive juniper scrub, grading into moorland and acid grassland. Birds likely to be seen in this area include both Black and Red Grouse, Golden Plover, Curlew, Snipe, Merlin, Short-eared Owl, Wheatear and possibly Twite. Netted Mountain Moth can be found on bearberry heath and Green Hairstreaks are present on some lower slopes.

Female Ptarmigan *I. Francis*

Glen Girnock (NO 325 957)

Glen Girnock showing regeneration *I. Francis*

Location & access: Situated south of the Dee between Ballater and Balmoral, Glen Girnock (**4**) was once a thriving area with several small farming settlements, but is now largely deserted. From Ballater take the South Deeside road (B976) west for approximately 6km to where an old bridge crosses the Girnock at the small hamlet of Littlemill. On the left is a rough grassy triangle between the trees with enough parking for 6-7 cars (**NO 325 957**). A bulldozed track marked *"Private road. Locked deer gate ahead"* leads south past a few occupied houses. Take this (crossing the stile) as far as wished along the glen and then return the same way, though a circular walk of some 14km is possible.

Habitat and potential wildlife: The walk starts in a mixed wood, largely Scots Pine and birch, with grassy clearings giving a woodland edge effect. It continues past conifer plantations, which have been deliberately screened by deciduous trees. Among the best places to scan for birds are the high wire fences along the side of the path. The track then opens out into an area of open moorland with plantation to the south and heather to the north.

Mid-May to mid-July is the best time to see the breeding birds. The woods are full of finches and tits, also Great Spotted Woodpecker, Jay and Song Thrush. Migrants include Willow Warbler, Whitethroat and Blackcap. Cuckoos can be heard calling from near the stream, and Buzzards and Ravens are often wheeling above. As the path opens out, you may see Spotted Flycatcher hunting from the wire fence and Tree Pipit displaying above the trees. The moor holds Meadow Pipit, Wheatear and the occasional Red Grouse, with Black Grouse also possible. The ruined farmstead of Loinveg (3km from the start) is certainly worth a visit. The tall trees and tumbled down walls usually attract Redstart, Siskin, Bullfinch and Mistle Thrush. Swallows nest in the outbuildings. After a good search here and possibly a picnic perched on the stones overlooking the valley, many birdwatchers will turn back at this point.

Wheatear *P. Newman*

However, a longer walk through wild deserted moorland is possible. Continue for another 2km as far as the ruins of Bovaglie (**NO 302 920**). Here, beside what was once the grandest house in the glen, you will be rewarded with wonderful views of the north side of Lochnagar. There are plenty of woodland birds in the trees around the house, such as Redpolls. The moorland can hold Stonechat and Whinchat, the latter now scarce. On fine summer days you may be lucky enough to see an adder basking on the sandy track, quickly disappearing into the heather on approach – this is one of the best areas in Deeside for this snake.

Stonechat *G. Holm*

The walk is worth doing at any time because of its varied habitat. Many of the woodland birds are present throughout the year, and over the moorland area various raptors such as Merlin and Golden Eagle have been recorded. Mammals include Roe and Red Deer, as well as Red Squirrels.

Glen Muick (NO 30 85)

Location & access: Glen Muick is a long glen extending south-west from Ballater some 15km to Loch Muick. A minor road allows access to the **Spittal of Glenmuick** (**5a**) (**NO 308 850**), where there is a ranger and visitor centre (www.balmoralcastle.com/ranger.htm) and toilets. A charge is made for parking here. It is possible to park carefully at various places along the road and take tracks or footpaths for walks, though the Spittal of Glenmuick offers the best all-round starting point. A circular walk can be taken around **Loch Muick** (**5b**) (**NO 29 83**) and the western end of the loch allows access to high level walks and to the **Dubh Loch** (**5c**) (**NO 23 82**).

Upper Loch Muick towards Dubh Loch *P. Grant*

Habitat and potential wildlife: The variety of habitats here offers a wide range of wildlife. The open moorland, grasslands and bogs hold Red Grouse, Black Grouse (which can be numerous and can often be seen from the road and around the visitor centre), Curlew, Snipe, Woodcock, Golden Plover, Lapwing, Greylag Goose and Wheatear. Ospreys sometimes fly up the glen to the loch and Golden Eagles can be seen, usually high overhead. The woodlands can hold crossbills (check for different species) and Long-eared Owl. Loch Muick, the largest loch in North-East Scotland, is clear and nutrient poor, but can hold Goosanders and sometimes divers. Common Gulls and Common Sandpipers nest by the loch. Ring Ouzels can be heard high above the loch and Peregrine and Merlin may be encountered. The whole glen holds large numbers of Red Deer, which can be seen at close quarters, especially in the autumn when rutting takes place. Roe Deer are also widespread. Mountain Hares are often seen from the minor road.

Lochnagar (NO 24 85)

Location & access: Lochnagar (**6**) is a very high mountain (1,155m) offering spectacular views and arctic-alpine habitats. It is only around 7km to the top from the Spittal of Glenmuick using the most direct route, though the ascent is strenuous. It is worth remembering that the weather can be hostile at any time of year and suitable clothing, equipment and navigational skills are essential.

The most common approach is from the Spittal of Glenmuick in a circuit via Glas-allt Shiel at the western end of Loch Muick. The high-level plateau extending south-west from the summit allows easy access to other Munros towards Glen Clunie. There are other ways of ascending the mountain, all involving much longer walks. Spring and summer are the most rewarding seasons; winter walks here do offer spectacular scenery but the range of species likely to be seen is much reduced.

Lochnagar from the Spittal of Glenmuick *P. Grant*

Habitat and potential wildlife: The main interest lies in the arctic-alpine species and habitats. The area is designated as a Special Protection Area for birds and holds the full range of species that can be expected in Scottish high montane environments. These include Ptarmigan, Dotterel, Snow Bunting, Wheatear, Golden Plover, Dunlin, Peregrine, Raven and eagles (both Golden and White-tailed can be seen). Many arctic-alpine plants are present and Mountain Hare and Red Deer are widespread.

Golden Eagle *E. Weston*

Braemar Area

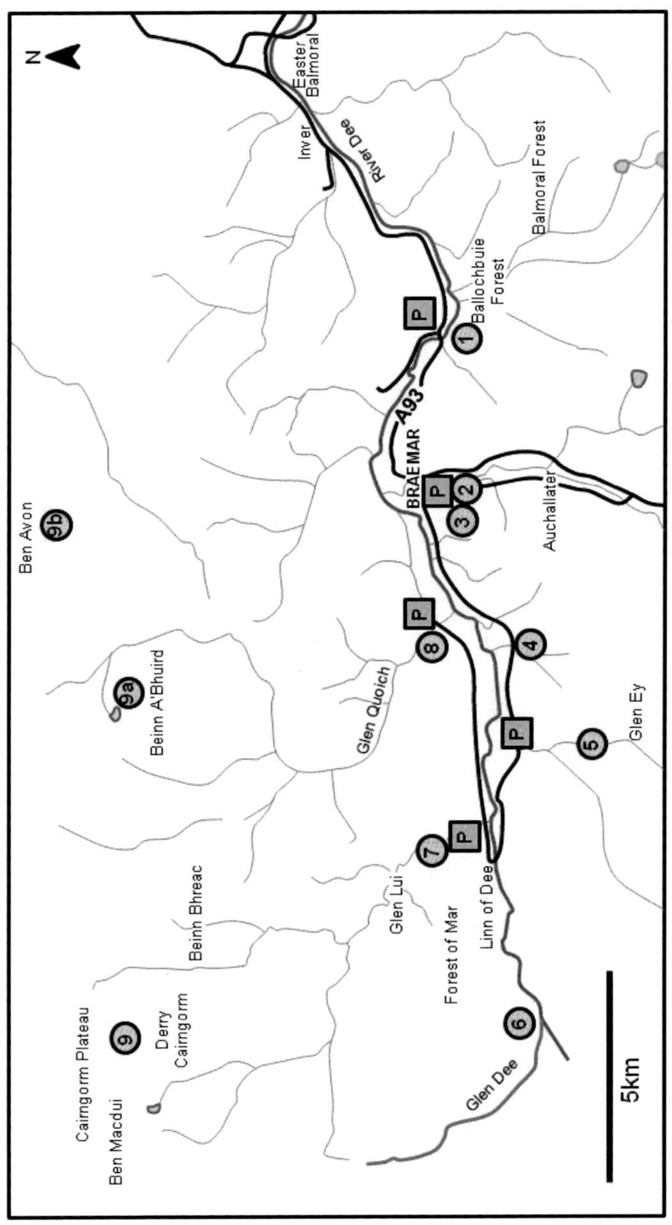

From arctic-alpine mountain tops to valley floors, from Birch and Juniper to ancient pine woods, from heather-clad hillsides to large rivers and small streams, the habitats around Braemar are extremely varied. Glaciers have carved out much of the landscape as evidenced by the U-shaped valleys. Spring and summer are the best times for bird watchers, though some of the characteristic species here are resident.

Ballochbuie Forest (NO 19 90)

Ballochbuie Forest *I. Francis*

Location & access: The easiest access to this forest is from the car park at Keiloch on the Invercauld Estate (**NO 189 913**) north of the main road; cross the A93 and the old General Wade bridge over the Dee, entering the forest through the gate (**1**). Other routes are possible from the east near Balmoral Castle. There is a network of paths and track within the forest, some of which can form circular routes.

Habitat and potential wildlife: Ballochbuie is a large and spectacular Caledonian pine forest occupying the lower northern slopes of Lochnagar. The breeding birds of the forest and adjacent areas include Black Grouse, Sparrowhawk, Buzzard, Merlin, Woodcock, Green Woodpecker, Tree Pipit, Redstart, Jay, Raven and all three crossbill species. Capercaillie is now very rare in all upper Deeside woodlands, including those in the Ballochbuie area. There are many Red Deer outside the fenced parts of the forest, Red Squirrels are frequent and Pine Martens are now widespread, as in most other woods in Deeside. The River Dee to the north of the forest holds Goosander, Dipper,

Grey Wagtail and Common Sandpiper. Ospreys can sometimes be seen flying along the river and it is always worth scanning the hilltops and sky between Ballater and Braemar for Golden Eagles.

Braemar Village (NO 150 914)

Before setting off for the better known upland areas, it is worthwhile spending some time around the village of Braemar, where a range of birds and plants can be seen, and where there is accommodation, shops and toilets.

Location & access: park in the village, and follow Cluniebank Rd (the "Old Military Road") southwards along the River Clunie to Braemar golf course (**2**).

Habitat and potential wildlife: The village provides a range of species, and the route leads to open countryside. Check the breeding colonies of House Martin, Swallow, Swift and Jackdaw in Braemar itself. The river is home to Mallard, Dipper, Pied and Grey Wagtail while the fields and gardens to the west can be occupied by Song and Mistle Thrush, Blackbird, tits, and finches including Greenfinch, Chaffinch and the occasional Brambling. Once beyond the golf course (beware of golfers playing across the road), the glen opens out. A quarry on the right has a nesting colony of Sand Martins. Lapwing, Curlew, Oystercatcher, Common and Black-headed Gull are present in the low grounds opposite throughout the breeding season with Buzzard frequently overhead.

Another nearby area, south-west of the village, is the **Morrone Birkwood** (**3**) (**NO 140 908**), a National Nature Reserve. Leaving the village centre car park, follow Chapel Brae to the wood. Black Grouse, Cuckoo, Tree Pipit, Stonechat and Siskin can all occur. The area is of particular interest to botanists. The wood is a Special Area of Conservation due to its flora developed on calcareous soils and adjacent acidic soil. It contains the most extensive and diverse example of a transition between woodland and juniper scrub in the UK. Juniper is actively regenerating above the birch woodland. Significant plants include

Dee floodplain and Morrone Birkwood *I. Francis*

Twinflower, Serrated Wintergreen, Interrupted Clubmoss, Nodding Melick, Globeflower, and Northern Bedstraw also occurs.

Mar Lodge and Mar Estates - Linn of Dee (NO 063 897) and Glen Quoich (NO 118 911)

Location & access: Leaving Braemar, follow the Linn of Dee road westwards, along the River Dee floodplain. This gives access to a fantastic area for wildlife with mature pine forest and moorland. Various car parks are available, at Inverey, Linn of Dee and Glen Quoich, at the start of each walk.

Habitat and potential wildlife: The National Trust for Scotland's Mar Lodge Estate covers an enormous area of land extending to 29,000ha (www.nts.org.uk/property/mar-lodge-estate) and to the south-east lies the smaller Mar Estate. Lower-lying areas here are heavily forested, and this landscape of native woodland and planted pine and broadleaved forest holds breeding crossbills (all three species are possible in the Forest of Mar area), Redstart, Tree Pipit, Spotted Flycatcher, Jay, Woodcock, Cuckoo, Long-eared Owl, Green Woodpecker, Black Grouse and Goosander. It is worth noting that Crested Tits do not occur anywhere in Deeside, except as very rare occasional visitors. Open country is quartered by raptors including eagles, while waders and gulls on the wet flushes and marshy floodplain are common. Red Squirrels, Red and Roe Deer are easily seen, and Pine Martens are becoming more common.

Between Braemar village and **Linn of Dee** (**NO 062 897**) are a few stopping points worth exploring. Two lay-bys offering panoramic views over the River Dee are ideal for photographing the Cairngorm high tops and the upper Dee valley, as well as scanning for eagles. Just before the Corriemulzie bridge (**4**) (**NO 113 892**) which spans a deep gorge, a 0.5km track leads southwards towards a disused dam once serving an earlier incarnation of Mar Lodge. Grey and Pied Wagtail and other passerines are found here, with both dragonflies and damselflies abundant.

A large car park (**NO 088 892**) in the hamlet of Inverey is the start of a well-worn track south into spectacular **Glen Ey** (**5**) on the Mar Estate, at the head of which are the ruins of Altanour Lodge. En-route, depending on the season, Ravens, Cuckoos, thrushes and raptors are regularly spotted. At Piper's Wood, planted within the last 25 years, is a thriving Adder population. Glen Ey also holds a population of Mountain Hares. A historical and geological feature in the glen is the Colonel's Bed gorge. Care is needed to descend the slope to the concealed rock formations.

River Dee at White Bridge *P. Grant*

The most popular car park (**NO 063 897**) is set back in woods on the north side of the River Dee, 300m beyond the bridge at the **Linn of Dee**. From the bridge Salmon can be seen leaping en-route to their spawning grounds. There is a choice to head westwards from the bridge; a vehicle track on the north side (easier going and recommended) and a narrow track south of the river. Both head towards White Bridge (**6**) and the Chest of Dee and thereafter, after a strenuous walk, to the source of the river high on Braeriach. Along the river Common Sandpipers can be seen while Goosanders regularly fly past. Wheatears are plentiful. Meadow Pipits and Skylarks form a large proportion of the rare Merlin's diet. Keep an eye on the sky for other raptors.

A third path takes you northwards through the car park to the River Lui (**7**). Crossbills are found here and other woodland species including Black Grouse. Jay, Tawny Owl, Woodcock, Wren, Robin and Dunnock can also be heard or seen all year but in harsh conditions most tend to disappear downstream. Dipper will however remain as long as ice does not cover the entire river surface. In summer look out for Tree Pipit and Redstart, with an outside chance of Pied Flycatcher.

View north across Dee floodplain to the Quoich *P. Grant*

Glen Quoich (**8**) (**NO 118 911**) lies 3km beyond the spectacular Mar Lodge, again on the north side of the River Dee. Excellent walks can start from here, either eastwards along the track towards Invercauld Estate or northwards up Glen Quoich. The woods hold migrants such as Redstart, Willow Warbler and Chiffchaff. A variety of raptors, including Golden Eagle, find this area productive, with Buzzard and Peregrine the most evident. Looking across the Dee floodplain will give views of breeding waders, Curlew, Lapwing and Oystercatcher being the most obvious. Here, ditch blocking and other management work by the estates has resulted in wetter conditions and an increase in breeding numbers of some waders and colonisation by other wetland species such as Water Rail, Sedge and Grasshopper Warblers. Recently, Greylag Geese have begun to breed here.

Lapwing *P. Newman*

The Cairngorms tops (9) (NN 99 99 area), Beinn a' Bhuird (9a) (NO 09 98) and Ben Avon (9b) (NO 13 01)

Location & access: Although frequently associated with Speyside (from where access is easier), the high tops of the Cairngorms are shared with Moray and Deeside, and indeed the River Dee rises at the Wells of Dee at 1,050m on Braeriach. Some extensive areas of the wider Cairngorm plateau lie in Aberdeenshire and there are numerous possible long walking routes in from the south. The car parks on Mar Lodge Estate are the most usual starting points for the Cairngorms (see Linn of Dee above). The large and spectacular high-level ridges and tors of Beinn a' Bhuird and Ben Avon are most easily accessed from the same car parks, or from the Keiloch car park (**NO 189 913**), next to Ballochbuie forest on the Invercauld Estate.

Beinn a' Bhuird from Ben Avon *P. Grant*

Habitat and potential wildlife: One of the most renowned areas for wildlife and natural habitats in the country, the arctic-alpine plateau in the Cairngorm Mountains holds a specialised community of birds which breed only in such high montane areas of Scotland. Ptarmigan are widespread and there are smaller numbers of Dotterel and Snow Bunting. Snowy Owls have even been present in spring or summer in several years, but breeding has never taken place. Although long walks are needed to explore many parts of the central Cairngorms and the plateaux on Beinn a' Bhuird and Ben Avon, and camping is worth considering, the effort is always worthwhile. Other birds that can be encountered include Golden Eagle, Peregrine, Raven, Ring Ouzel, Golden Plover, Dunlin, Common Gull, Common Sandpiper, Wheatear and Meadow Pipit.

Snow Bunting *I. Francis*

Dotterel *I. Francis*

Red Deer and Mountain Hare are widespread (though not numerous everywhere) and on Ben Macdui the semi-tame herd of Reindeer from Glen More can sometimes be seen! On cliff faces and in flushes, there are many highly localised montane plants, mosses and liverworts, and most of the plant communities are distinctive and confined to these high altitude areas within the British Isles. Several specialist mountain moths can be found, including Scotch Burnet, Black Mountain Moth, Broad-bordered White Underwing and Northern Dart.

Glen Clunie area, Glen Callater, The Cairnwell (Glen Shee Ski Area) and the Mounth Hills

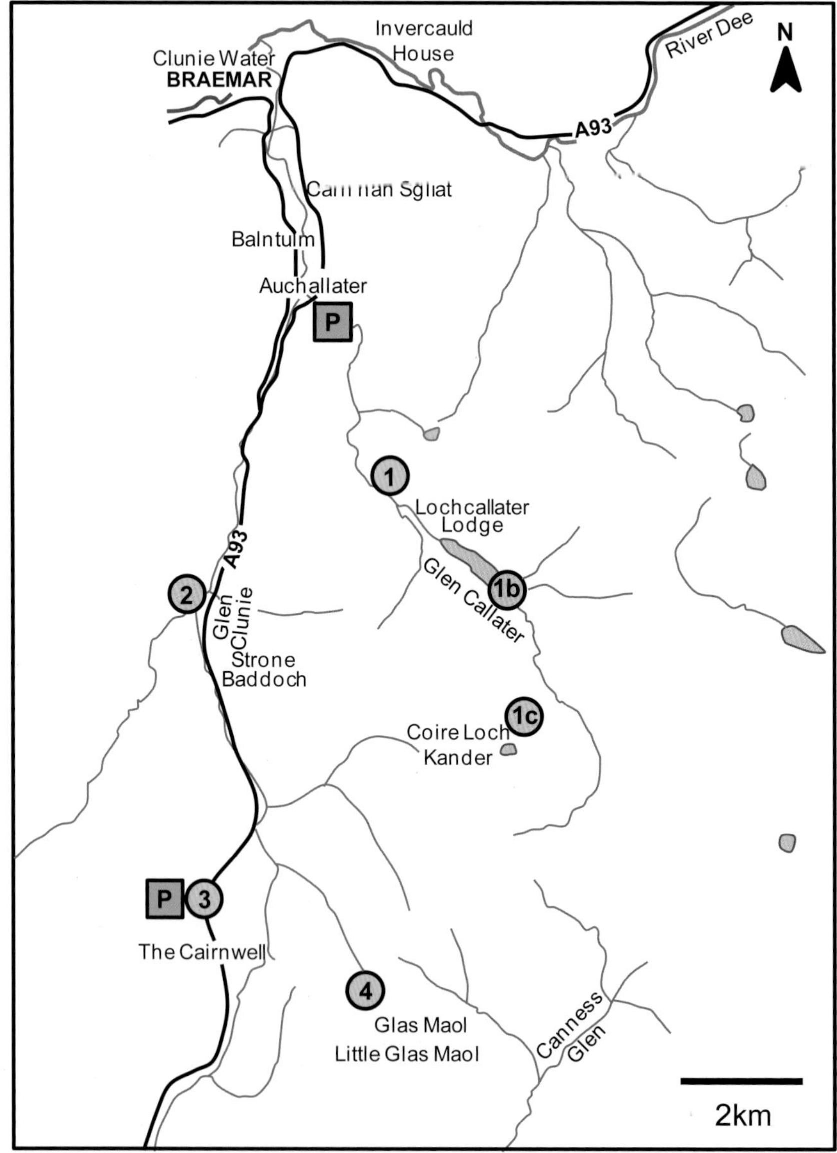

Location & access: The following sites can be accessed from the A93, south of Braemar. Parking is available at several sites along the route, and open country and high mountain paths give access to a range of habitats.

Loch Callater *P. Grant*

Habitat and potential wildlife: The A93 leads through upland moorland and mountain scenery, with the road reaching 665m, the highest road in Britain at Glen Shee ski centre. In winter large herds (often over 1,000) of Red Deer are often seen at close quarters. White Mountain Hares can be seen, along with Red Grouse at the side of the road. **Glen Callater** (**1**) can be accessed from Auchallater (**NO 156 882**) and is worth a walk for a range of uplands birds (Adder also possible), and the loch (NO 18 84) can hold Wigeon and Goosander, both of which breed in the area. The corries above the loch (such as **Coire Kander**, **NO 190 810** (**1c**)) hold a diverse range of arctic-alpine plants; the whole of the Glen Clunie area is underlain by base-rich rocks providing good conditions for plant growth.

Loch Kander *P. Grant*

Ring Ouzel *P. Newman*

Glen Clunie, the conifer plantation at Baddoch (**2**) (**NO 138 834**) is a good place to pause or walk into the hills to the west. Sparrowhawk and Kestrel are often seen above the wood with Fieldfare and Redwing finding productive feeding grounds further along the track. Ring Ouzels are also widely present in this upland habitat, which holds a stable population of several tens of pairs.

Around the **Glen Shee Ski Centre** (**3**) (**NO 138 781**) car park, Snow Bunting can be seen foraging in winter, while, with the benefit of a telescope, Ptarmigan (especially in winter) can be spotted higher up the slopes where Raven also gather. The A93 at the ski area is the highest main road in Scotland at 665m; here it crosses **the Mounth** – a range of high hills that stretches for some 60km eastwards to south of Banchory. It is a short, though steep, ascent to the mountain tops on both sides of the ski area. Walking east towards **Glas Maol** (**4**) (**NO 166 766**) in summer can produce typical upland breeding birds including Wheatear, Golden Plover and Dunlin, whilst the scree slopes hold Ptarmigan, and in May/June trips of Dotterel might be encountered. In fact, the area encompassing most of the high tops of the Mounth, from Beinn Iutharn Mhor (**NO 04 79**) east past An Socach (**NO 08 80**), across to Carn an Tuirc (**NO 18 80**) and Broad Cairn (**NO 23 81**) offers a chance to encounter Dotterel throughout the summer. The sites most easily accessible from the Ski Centre can be very disturbed by walkers (and dogs), and it is recommended that when visiting the high tops you start early and avoid weekends. Always be aware of the conditions and be prepared for rapidly varying weather.

Snow Bunting *R. Humphreys*

Dunlin *I. Francis*

Glas Maol from Glen Shee car park *P. Grant*

6. DONSIDE AND UPPER DEVERON AREA

The Lecht Ski Centre and the Ladder Hills (NJ 27 19)

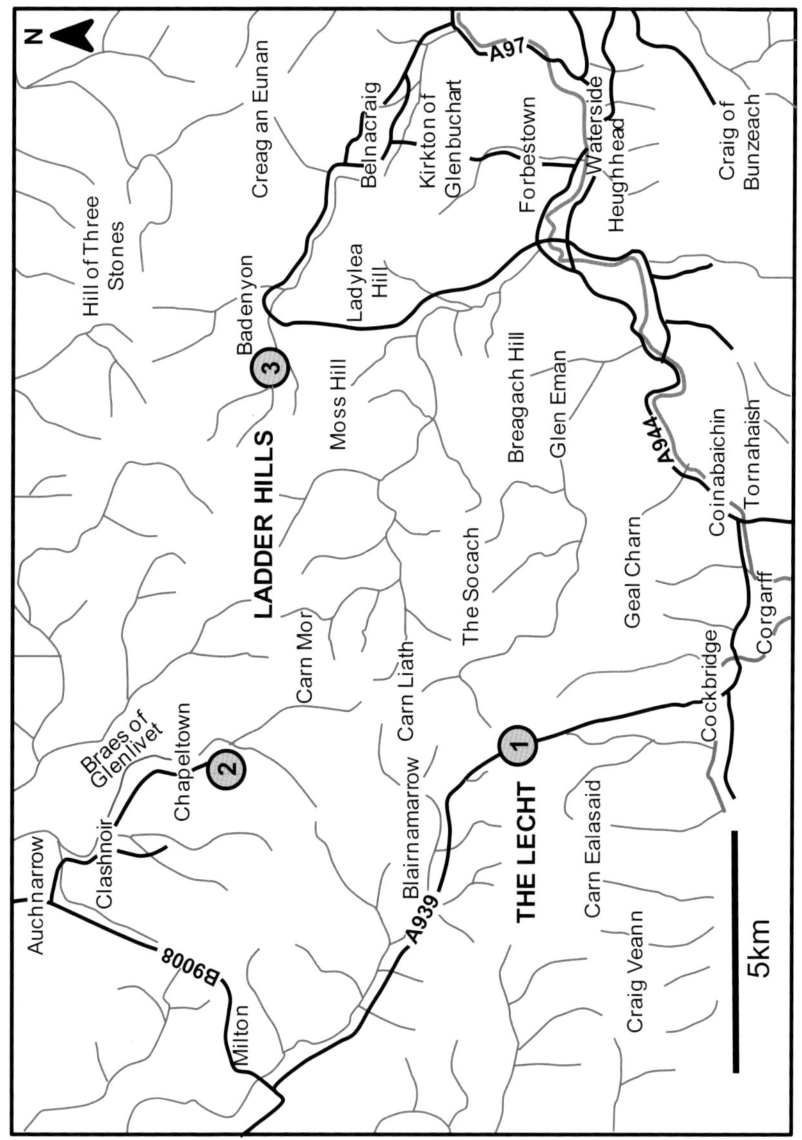

Location & access: Forming the border between Aberdeenshire and Moray, the Ladder Hills are a lower altitude, north-eastern extension of the Cairngorms and offer commanding views over the whole north-east. Though nowhere near as high (700-800m), the rounded, peat and moorland dominated summits are wind-swept and hold wind-clipped heath and bog pools. The easiest starting point for exploration is **The Lecht Ski Centre** (**1**) (**NJ 247 129**), situated on the A939, Britain's second highest major road at 644m – and often blocked by snow in winter. The hills to the south-west and north-east are accessible from here. The ascent is steep and weather conditions can be severe. Other access points are possible from the **Braes of Glenlivet** (**2**) (**NJ 254 204**) to the north in Moray and from **Glenbuchat** (**3**) (**NJ 335 186**).

Ladder Hills looking east from Carn Liath *I. Francis*

Redshank display *G. Holm*

Habitat and potential wildlife: Lapwing, Curlew, Snipe with scattered Redshank and Black Grouse breed in the wet grassland and rough grazing land at lower levels while Red Grouse, abundant Golden Plover and rarer Dunlin nest among the wet bogs and pools of the higher ground. Burns hold Dipper, Grey Wagtail and Common Sandpiper. Breeding raptors include Merlin and Hen Harrier when they are undisturbed. There is a chance of Golden Eagle and Peregrine, along with Wheatear and Ring Ouzel.

Several small Common Gull colonies are found, especially near the Lecht. At the Ski Centre, Snow Buntings can often be seen around the car parks in winter and Ravens (sometimes flocks of up to 20 birds) scavenge the roads for traffic casualty Mountain Hares. The hares can be abundant here, though numbers have declined due to shooting on driven grouse estates.

Clashindarroch and Cabrach area

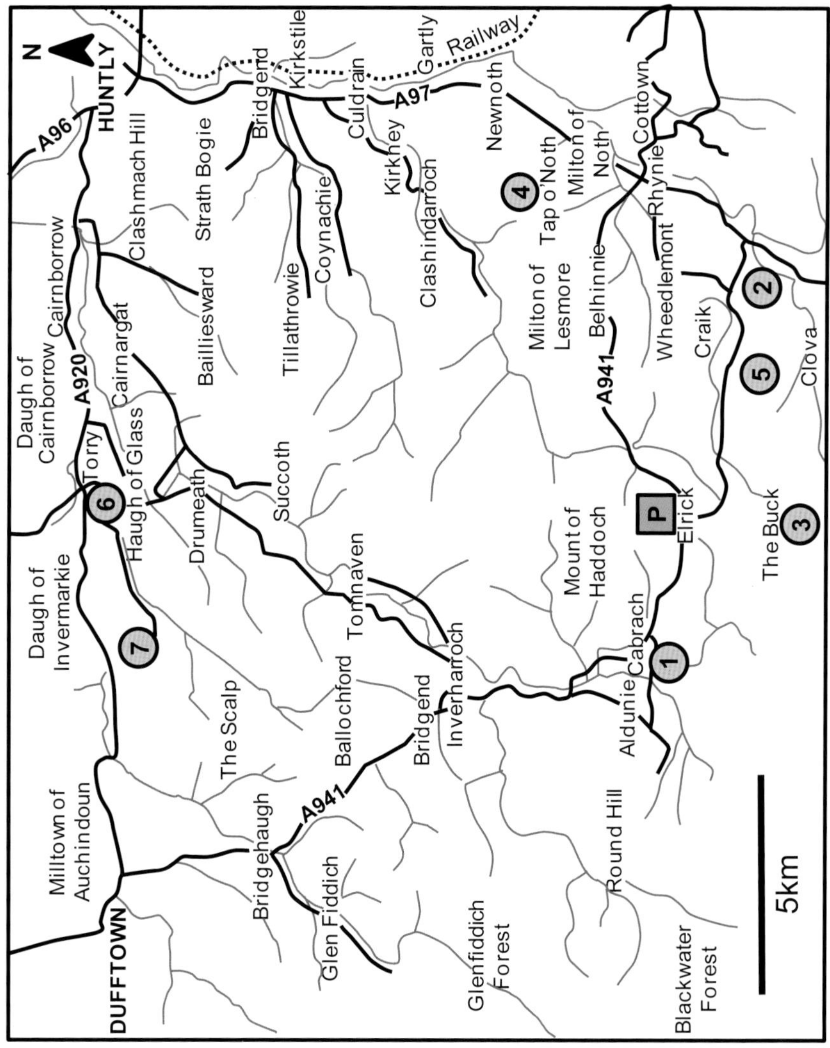

Location & access: The Forestry Commission's **Clashindarroch Forest** (**NJ 43 29**) is one of the largest planted coniferous forests in North-East Scotland. There is an extensive network of tracks and in winter a cross-country skiing course. The ski car park (**P**) at **NJ 430 270** provides a good starting point. It is surrounded to the west and south by open moorland and upland farmland around the **Cabrach** (**1**) (**NJ 38 29**) and towards **Craig Castle** near Rhynie (**2**). The A941 Rhynie to Dufftown road crosses the area and provides a good vantage point to view the area. Side roads and footpaths offer the chance to explore. An ascent of **The Buck** (**3**) (**NJ 412 235; 721m**) is rewarded by panoramic views and the **Tap o'Noth vitrified hill fort** (**4**) (**NJ 484 293**) also gives extensive views over the forest.

Clashindarroch Forest *I. Francis*

Habitat and potential wildlife: This is a remote upland landscape, with a mosaic of forest, heather moorland, bogs, fens and enclosed farmland – mostly grassland but some arable crops. A wide range of species can be seen here, many present only in spring and summer. The forest holds crossbills, Siskin, Sparrowhawk, Woodcock, Tree Pipit, Buzzard, Tawny Owl, Long-eared Owl and there is a chance of Goshawk. The surrounding moorland and farmland holds breeding waders such as Lapwing, Curlew, Oystercatcher and Snipe in good numbers. Hen Harrier and Short-eared Owl are likely in good years (though both are rare), with Merlin and Peregrine also possible. Red

Red Grouse *I. Francis*

Grouse and Black Grouse are found, along with scattered Ring Ouzel and Twite in steeper valleys. The rivers hold Common Sandpiper, Goosander and Grey Wagtail with scattered breeding Common Gulls. Red and Roe Deer are present in quite high numbers, with low densities of Mountain Hares. Clashindarroch Forest area holds Pine Marten, Red Squirrel and the possibility of Scottish Wildcat (but also hybrid cats). The **Hill of Towanreef** area (**5**) (**NJ 45 24**) is a Special Area of Conservation for its specialised geology and flora. The rocks here are formed from serpentine, and produce conditions rich in metals, which restrict the plants that grow here to tolerant specialists such as Spring Sandwort. This leads to bare areas of rock and soil, and oddities such as the normally maritime Thrift growing alongside the roads. Most of the flushes and grasslands in the area have a rich and colourful flora.

Glass and the Tips of Corsemaul

Location & access: The A920 Huntly to Dufftown road straddles the headwaters of the rivers Bogie and Deveron, and passes through **Glass** (**6**) (**NJ 42 39**) and over the **Tips of Corsemaul** (**7**) (**NJ 39 39**). It provides a good opportunity to view the moorlands, fields and woodlands of this attractive upland area. Walks can be taken along minor roads and tracks in the area.

Tips of Corsemaul Gullery *I. Francis*

Habitat and potential wildlife: The Haugh of Glass is a mosaic of coniferous and deciduous woodlands, farmland, river and semi-natural grassland and heath. The Tips of Corsemaul lies on moorland with flushes, and scattered pine and broadleaved trees, with enclosed farmland along the roadside. This mix of habitats offers a good range of upland species, most of which are only present in the spring and summer. Lapwing, Oystercatcher, Curlew and Snipe are widespread as breeders. Tree Pipit, Cuckoo and Spotted Flycatcher are present in the woodlands along the river, and Ospreys can be seen fishing in this area downstream to Huntly. On the scrubby moorland edges, there are breeding waders, Red Grouse, Stonechat, Grasshopper Warbler, Reed Bunting, Lesser Redpoll, and Merlin is possible. The main feature of interest in this area though is the largest colony of breeding Common Gulls in the UK, spread over several hilltops from **Tom Mor** (**NJ 40 38**) over the **Tips of Corsemaul** itself to the **Hill of Mackalea** (**NJ 37 38**). Though it has declined greatly since its peak at around 20,000 pairs in the late 1980s, there are still several thousand pairs present. The colony can be easily viewed from the road. There are also still a few Lesser Black-backed Gulls present, but again their numbers, along with those of Herring Gull (now gone) have declined greatly. The colony is designated as a Special Protection Area. There are good densities of breeding Curlew each side of the road at Tips of Corsemaul.

Lord's Throat, Bennachie and Monymusk

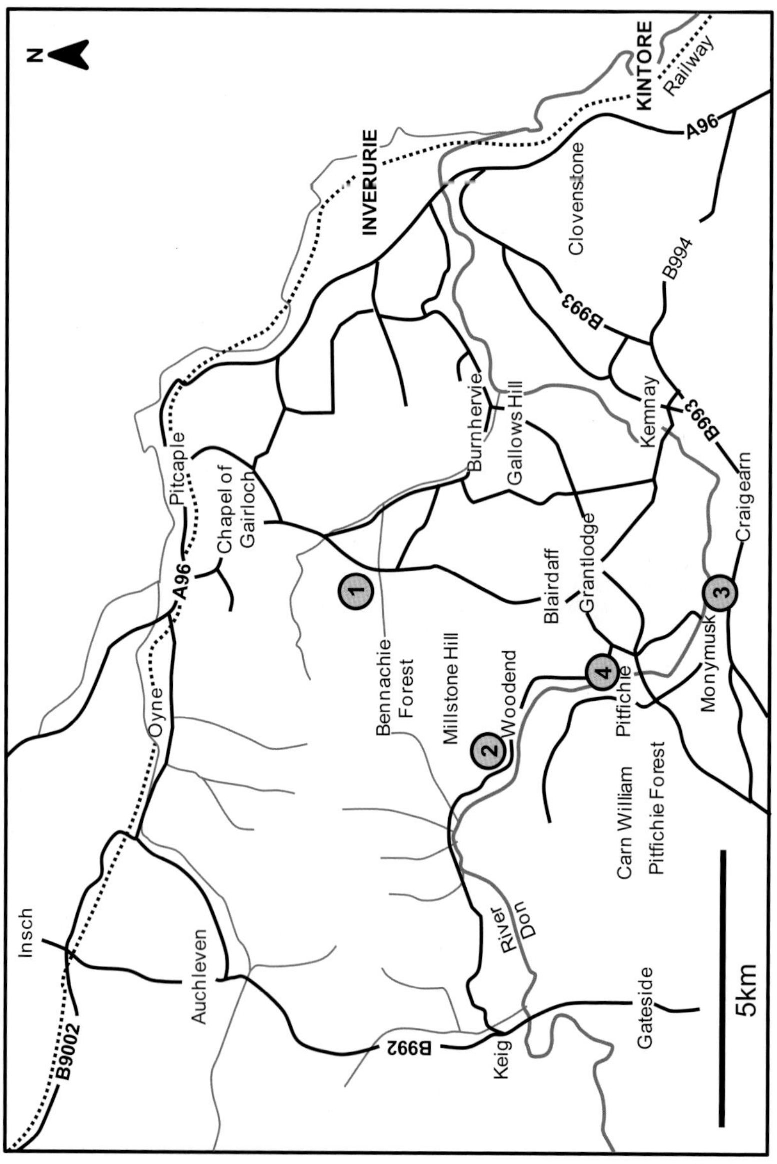

Location & access: The River Don flows eastwards through the **Lord's Throat** (**NJ 63 19**), south of the **Bennachie massif** (**NJ 68 22**) and past **Monymusk village** (**NJ 68 15**). Together, this area contains an attractive mix of upland and lowland habitats. There are many potential access points and walks (particularly through the various Forestry Commission woodlands) and a hotel in Monymusk. The **Bennachie Visitor Centre** (**1**) (**NJ 696 217**) provides wildlife viewing at feeders and much information about the wildlife of the area. This is a good access point for the steep climb to **Mither Tap** (**NJ 682 223; 518m**), a hill fort which has spectacular views over much of eastern Aberdeenshire. The **Woodend / Donview car park** (**2**) gives access to Millstone Hill, the river and woodland.

Bennachie Plateau *P. Grant*

Habitat and potential wildlife: The River Don here has Goosander, Common Sandpiper, Goldeneye and Grey Wagtail. This area is good for watching Ospreys fishing in summer. Woodlands have a good range of warblers, Redstart, Tree Pipit, Spotted Flycatcher, Green Woodpecker, Stock Dove and Woodcock. Buzzards are common and Goshawk and Red Kite may be seen, the latter especially nearer **Monymusk** (**3**). Moorland areas have Red Grouse, Merlin and Peregrine, and conifer forests hold crossbills and Siskin. There are breeding waders (Lapwing, Oystercatcher and Curlew) on the farmland, with Greylag Geese on ponds. In winter, there is often a large herd of Whooper Swans and a few Mute Swans on oilseed rape fields near **Pitfichie Castle** (**4**)(**NJ 683 163**). Red Squirrels are widespread in the woodlands and Brown Hares common in the fields.

Whooper Swans *I. Francis*

South-east of Monymusk, towards Kemnay, the National Trust for Scotland's property at **Castle Fraser** (**NJ 722 126**) is worth visiting for woodland walks with a wide range of birds and several ponds which are very rich in invertebrates, including butterflies. Azure Damselfly (scarce this far north) and the rare Northern Damselfly both occur. Red Kites can also be seen in the area.

Checklist of birds recorded in North-East Scotland

This checklist has been compiled by Paul Baxter, and is an update and re-working of the list produced by I. Phillips in 1997 *(Rare and Scarce Birds in North East Scotland)*. New taxonomic relationships and a new taxonomic order have been incorporated into the list.

In the intervening 17 years an additional 46 species have been recorded and accepted and are included in the new checklist. As always as soon as such a list is completed it is out of date, with four more species awaiting official acceptance from 2013 and January 2014. The list stands currently at 386 and, given the current rate of addition of new species, it cannot be long before the 400th species of bird is found.

Paul is thanked for permission to reproduce his list here. It is hoped that the inclusion of the "status" column will give an idea of the time of year that any particular species may be found, and indicates breeding potential.

The Status is indicated as following, and is based on that used in the Annual Reports:

V - vagrant: less than 20 records ever

R - rare: more than 20 records but not recorded annually

S - scarce: annual in small numbers (1 - 5 per year)

U - uncommon: normally found annually (5 - 50 records per year)

C - Common: easily and regularly encountered

The modifiers are given in lower case and indicate breeding, wintering or migration, as follows:

r - resident

b - breeding

s - summer

m - migrant

w - wintering

Thus Chiffchaff would be Cbm / Cm/ Sw - i.e. common breeding migrant, common migrant and scarce winter resident.

Species indicated with a **†** symbol are UK national rarities.

Species		Status	
Mute Swan	*Cygnus olor*	Cbr/Cm/Cw	
Bewick's Swan	*Cygnus columbianus*	Rm	
Whooper Swan	*Cygnus cygnus*	Cm/Cw	
Bean Goose	*Anser fabalis*	Um	
Pink-footed Goose	*Anser brachyrhynchus*	Cm/Cw	
White-fronted Goose	*Anser albifrons*	Um/Uw	
Greylag Goose	*Anser anser*	Ubr/Cw	
Snow Goose	*Anser caerulescens*	Rm	
Greater Canada Goose	*Branta canadensis*	Sbr/Um	
Barnacle Goose	*Branta leucopsis*	Cm/Cw	
Brent Goose	*Branta bernicla*	Um/Uw	
Red-breasted Goose†	*Branta ruficollis*	V	
Egyptian Goose	*Alopochen aegyptiaca*	V	
Shelduck	*Tadorna tadorna*	Cbr/Cm/Cw	
Mandarin Duck	*Aix galericulata*	Rbr/Um	
Wigeon	*Anas penelope*	Rbr/Cm/Cw	
American Wigeon	*Anas americana*	Rm	
Gadwall	*Anas strepera*	Rbm/Cm/Cw	
Teal	*Anas crecca*	Sbr/Cm/Cw	
Green-winged Teal	*Anas carolinensis*	V	
Mallard	*Anas platyrhynchos*	Cbr/Cm/Cw	
Black Duck †	*Anas rubripes*	V	
Pintail	*Anas acuta*	Cm/Cw	
Garganey	*Anas querquedula*	Rbm/Um	
Blue-winged Teal†	*Anas discors*	V	
Shoveler	*Anas clypeata*	Rbm/Cm/Cw	
Red-crested Pochard	*Netta rufina*	V	
Pochard	*Aythya ferina*	Rbm/Cm/Cw	
Ring-necked Duck	*Aythya collaris*	V	
Ferruginous Duck	*Aythya nyroca*	V	
Tufted Duck	*Aythya fuligula*	Cbr/Cm/Cw	
Scaup	*Aythya marila*	Um/Uw	
Lesser Scaup†	*Aythya affinis*	V	
Eider	*Somateria mollissima*	Cbr/Cm/Cw	
King Eider†	*Somateria spectabilis*	Rm	
Steller's Eider†	*Polysticta stelleri*	V	
Long-tailed Duck	*Clangula hyemalis*	Cm/Cw	
Common Scoter	*Melanitta nigra*	Cs /Cm /Cw	
Black Scoter†	*Melanitta americana*	V	
Surf Scoter	*Melanitta perspicillata*	Rm	
Velvet Scoter	*Melanitta fusca*	Um/Uw	
White-winged Scoter†	*Melanitta deglandi*	V	
Barrow's Goldeneye†	*Bucephala islandica*	V	
Goldeneye	*Bucephala clangula*	Ubr/Cm/Cw	
Smew	*Mergellus albellus*	Sm/Sw	
Red-breasted Merganser	*Mergus serrator*	Rbr/Cm/Cw	
Goosander	*Mergus merganser*	Ubr/Cm/Cw	
Ruddy Duck	*Oxyura jamaicensis*	V	
Quail	*Coturnix coturnix*	Rbm/Um	
Red-legged Partridge	*Alectoris rufa*	Cbr	
Red Grouse	*Lagopus lagopus*	Cbr	
Ptarmigan	*Lagopus muta*	Cbr	
Black Grouse	*Tetrao tetrix*	Ubr	
Capercaillie	*Tetrao urogallus*	Rbr	
Grey Partridge	*Perdix perdix*	Cbr	
Pheasant	*Phasianus colchicus*	Cbr	

Species		Status	
Red-throated Diver	*Gavia stellata*	Cm/Cw	
Black-throated Diver	*Gavia arctica*	Um/Uw	
Great Northern Diver	*Gavia immer*	Um/Uw	
White-billed Diver	*Gavia adamsii*	Rm	
Fulmar	*Fulmarus glacialis*	Cbr/Cm/Cw	
Cory's Shearwater	*Calonectris borealis*	Rm	
Great Shearwater	*Puffinus gravis*	Rm	
Sooty Shearwater	*Puffinus griseus*	Um	
Manx Shearwater	*Puffinus puffinus*	Cm	
Balearic Shearwater	*Puffinus mauretanicus*	Rm	
Storm Petrel	*Hydrobates pelagicus*	Cm	
Leach's Petrel	*Oceanodroma leucorhoa*	Um	
Swinhoe's Petrel †	*Oceanodroma monorhis*	V	
Gannet	*Morus bassanus*	Cbm/Cm/Cw	
Cormorant	*Phalacrocorax carbo*	Cbr/Cm/Cw	
Shag	*Phalacrocorax aristotelis*	Cbr/Cm/Cw	
Bittern	*Botaurus stellaris*	Um/Uw	
American Bittern†	*Botaurus lentiginosus*	V	
Little Bittern†	*Ixobrychus minutus*	V	
Night-heron	*Nycticorax nycticorax*	V	
Little Egret	*Egretta garzetta*	Um	
Great White Egret	*Ardea alba*	V	
Grey Heron	*Ardea cinerea*	Cbr/Cm/Cw	
Purple Heron	*Ardea purpurea*	V	
Black Stork†	*Ciconia nigra*	V	
White Stork	*Ciconia ciconia*	V	
Glossy Ibis	*Plegadis falcinellus*	V	
Spoonbill	*Platalea leucorodia*	Um	
Pied-billed Grebe†	*Podilymbus podiceps*	V	
Little Grebe	*Tachybaptus ruficollis*	Cbr/Cm/Cw	
Great Crested Grebe	*Podiceps cristatus*	Ubr/Um	
Red-necked Grebe	*Podiceps grisegena*	Rm	
Slavonian Grebe	*Podiceps auritus*	Um	
Black-necked Grebe	*Podiceps nigricollis*	Rm	
Honey-buzzard	*Pernis apivorus*	Rm	
Black Kite	*Milvus migrans*	V	
Red Kite	*Milvus milvus*	Cbr/Um/Cw	
White-tailed Eagle	*Haliaeetus albicilla*	Um	
Marsh Harrier	*Circus aeruginosus*	Um	
Hen Harrier	*Circus cyaneus*	Sbr/Um/Uw	
Pallid Harrier†	*Circus macrourus*	V	
Montagu's Harrier	*Circus pygargus*	V	
Goshawk	*Accipiter gentilis*	Ubr/Um/Uw	
Sparrowhawk	*Accipiter nisus*	Cbr/Cm/Cw	
Buzzard	*Buteo buteo*	Cbr/Cm/Cw	
Rough-legged Buzzard	*Buteo lagopus*	Rm/Rw	
Golden Eagle	*Aquila chrysaetos*	Ubr	
Osprey	*Pandion haliaetus*	Ub/Um	
Water Rail	*Rallus aquaticus*	Cbr/Cm/Cw	
Spotted Crake	*Porzana porzana*	Rbm/Rm	
Corncrake	*Crex crex*	Rbm/Rm	
Moorhen	*Gallinula chloropus*	Cbr/Cm/Cw	
Coot	*Fulica atra*	Cbr/Cm/Cw	
Crane	*Grus grus*	Rb/Um	
Sandhill Crane†	*Grus canadensis*	V	
Little Bustard†	*Tetrax tetrax*	V	
Macqueen's Bustard†	*Chlamydotis macqueenii*	V	

Species		Status	
Stone-curlew	*Burhinus oedicnemus*	V	
Black-winged Stilt†	*Himantopus himantopus*	V	
Avocet	*Recurvirostra avosetta*	Um	
Oystercatcher	*Haematopus ostralegus*	Cbr/Cm/Cw	
American Golden Plover	*Pluvialis dominica*	V	
Pacific Golden Plover†	*Pluvialis fulva*	V	
Golden Plover	*Pluvialis apricaria*	Cbr/Cm/Cw	
Grey Plover	*Pluvialis squatarola*	Cm/Cw	
Lapwing	*Vanellus vanellus*	Cbr/Cm/Cw	
Little Ringed Plover	*Charadrius dubius*	Rbm/Um	
Ringed Plover	*Charadrius hiaticula*	Cbr/Cm/Cw	
Killdeer†	*Charadrius vociferus*	V	
Kentish Plover	*Charadrius alexandrinus*	V	
Lesser Sand Plover†	*Charadrius mongolus*	V	
Greater Sand Plover†	*Charadrius leschenaultii*	V	
Dotterel	*Charadrius morinellus*	Cbm/Um	
Upland Sandpiper†	*Bartramia longicauda*	V	
Eskimo Curlew†	*Numenius borealis*	Extinct	
Whimbrel	*Numenius phaeopus*	Cm	
Curlew	*Numenius arquata*	Cbr/Cm/Cw	
Black-tailed Godwit	*Limosa limosa*	Cm	
Hudsonian Godwit†	*Limosa haemastica*	V	
Bar-tailed Godwit	*Limosa lapponica*	Cm/Cw	
Turnstone	*Arenaria interpres*	Cm/Cw	
Knot	*Calidris canutus*	Cm/Cw	
Ruff	*Calidris pugnax*	Cm	
Broad-billed Sandpiper†	*Calidris falcinellus*	V	
Curlew Sandpiper	*Calidris ferruginea*	Cm	
Stilt Sandpiper†	*Calidris himantopus*	V	
Temminck's Stint	*Calidris temminckii*	Rm	
Sanderling	*Calidris alba*	Cm/Cw	
Dunlin	*Calidris alpina*	Ubr/Cm/Cw	
Purple Sandpiper	*Calidris maritima*	Cm/Cw	
Baird's Sandpiper†	*Calidris bairdii*	V	
Little Stint	*Calidris minuta*	Cm	
White-rumped Sandpiper†	*Calidris fuscicollis*	Rm	
Least Sandpiper†	*Calidris minutilla*	V	
Buff-breasted Sandpiper†	*Calidris subruficollis*	Rm	
Pectoral Sandpiper	*Calidris melanotos*	Um	
Semipalmated Sandpiper†	*Calidris pusilla*	V	
Wilson's Phalarope†	*Phalaropus tricolor*	V	
Red-necked Phalarope	*Phalaropus lobatus*	Rm	
Grey Phalarope	*Phalaropus fulicarius*	Um	
Terek Sandpiper†	*Xenus cinereus*	V	
Common Sandpiper	*Actitis hypoleucos*	Cbm/Cm	
Green Sandpiper	*Tringa ochropus*	Cm	
Spotted Redshank	*Tringa erythropus*	Cm	
Greater Yellowlegs†	*Tringa melanoleuca*	V	
Greenshank	*Tringa nebularia*	Cm	
Lesser Yellowlegs†	*Tringa flavipes*	V	
Marsh Sandpiper†	*Tringa stagnatilis*	V	
Wood Sandpiper	*Tringa glareola*	Cm	
Redshank	*Tringa totanus*	Ubr/Cm/Cw	
Jack Snipe	*Lymnocryptes minimus*	Cm/Cw	
Short-billed Dowitcher†	*Limnodromus griseus*	V	
Long-billed Dowitcher†	*Limnodromus scolopaceus*	V	
Woodcock	*Scolopax rusticola*	Cbr/Cm/Cw	

Species		Status	
Snipe	*Gallinago gallinago*	Cbr/Cm/Cw	
Great Snipe†	*Gallinago media*	V	
Black-winged Pratincole†	*Glareola nordmanni*	V	
Pomarine Skua	*Stercorarius pomarinus*	Cm	
Arctic Skua	*Stercorarius parasiticus*	Cm	
Long-tailed Skua	*Stercorarius longicaudus*	Um	
Great Skua	*Stercorarius skua*	Cm	
Puffin	*Fratercula arctica*	Cbm/Cm/ Uw	
Black Guillemot	*Cepphus grylle*	Sbr/Uw	
Razorbill	*Alca torda*	Cbr/Cm/Cw	
Little Auk	*Alle alle*	Um/Uw	
Guillemot	*Uria aalge*	Cbr/Cm/Cw	
Brünnich's Guillemot †	*Uria lomvia*	V	
Bridled Tern†	*Onychoprion anaethetus*	V	
Little Tern	*Sternula albifrons*	Rbm/Um	
Caspian Tern†	*Hydroprogne caspia*	V	
Whiskered Tern†	*Chlidonias hybrida*	V	
Black Tern	*Chlidonias niger*	Um	
White-winged Black Tern	*Chlidonias leucopterus*	V	
Sandwich Tern	*Sterna sandvicensis*	Cbm/Cm	
Forster's Tern†	*Sterna forsteri*	V	
Common Tern	*Sterna hirundo*	Cbm/Cm	
Roseate Tern	*Sterna dougallii*	Um	
Arctic Tern	*Sterna paradisaea*	Cbm/Cm	
Ivory Gull†	*Pagophila eburnea*	V	
Sabine's Gull	*Xema sabini*	Rm	
Kittiwake	*Rissa tridactyla*	Cbr/Cm/Cw	
Bonaparte's Gull†	*Chroicocephalus philadelphia*	V	
Black-headed Gull	*Chroicocephalus ridibundus*	Cbr/Cm/Cw	
Little Gull	*Hydrocoloeus minutus*	Cm	
Ross's Gull†	*Rhodostethia rosea*	V	
Laughing Gull†	*Larus atricilla*	V	
Franklin's Gull†	*Larus pipixcan*	V	
Mediterranean Gull	*Larus melanocephalus*	Um/Uw	
Common Gull	*Larus canus*	Cbr/Cm/Cw	
Ring-billed Gull	*Larus delawarensis*	V	
Lesser Black-backed Gull	*Larus fuscus*	Ubm/Cm/Rw	
Herring Gull	*Larus argentatus*	Cbr/Cm/Cw	
Yellow-legged Gull	*Larus michahellis*	V	
Caspian Gull	*Larus cachinnans*	V	
Iceland Gull	*Larus glaucoides*	Um/Uw	
Glaucous Gull	*Larus hyperboreus*	Um/Uw	
Great Black-backed Gull	*Larus marinus*	Ubr/Cm/Cw	
Pallas's Sandgrouse†	*Syrrhaptes paradoxus*	V	
Rock Dove / Feral Pigeon	*Columba livia*	Cbr	
Stock Dove	*Columba oenas*	Cbr/Cw	
Woodpigeon	*Columba palumbus*	Cbr/Cm/Cw	
Collared Dove	*Streptopelia decaocto*	Cbr	
Turtle Dove	*Streptopelia turtur*	Rm	
Cuckoo	*Cuculus canorus*	Cbm/Um	
Barn Owl	*Tyto alba*	Ubr/Um	
Scops Owl †	*Otus scops*	V	
Snowy Owl†	*Bubo scandiacus*	V	
Hawk Owl †	*Surnia ulula*	V	
Little Owl†	*Athene noctua*	V	
Tawny Owl	*Strix aluco*	Cbr	
Long-eared Owl	*Asio otus*	Ubr/Um/Uw	

Species		Status	
Short-eared Owl	***Asio flammeus***	**Ubr/Um/Uw**	
Tengmalm's Owl †	***Aegolius funereus***	**V**	
Nightjar	***Caprimulgus europaeus***	**Rm**	
Swift	***Apus apus***	**Cbm/Cm**	
Pallid Swift†	***Apus pallidus***	**V**	
Alpine Swift	***Apus melba***	**V**	
Hoopoe	***Upupa epops***	**Rm**	
Bee-eater	***Merops apiaster***	**V**	
Roller †	***Coracias garrulus***	**V**	
Kingfisher	***Alcedo atthis***	**Ubr**	
Belted Kingfisher†	***Megaceryle alcyon***	**V**	
Wryneck	***Jynx torquilla***	**Um**	
Green Woodpecker	***Picus viridis***	**Ubr**	
Great Spotted Woodpecker	***Dendrocopos major***	**Cbr**	
Lesser Kestrel†	***Falco naumanni***	**V**	
Kestrel	***Falco tinnunculus***	**Cbr/Cm**	
Red-footed Falcon	***Falco vespertinus***	**V**	
Merlin	***Falco columbarius***	**Ubr/Um/Uw**	
Hobby	***Falco subbuteo***	**Um**	
Gyr Falcon †	***Falco rusticolus***	**V**	
Peregrine	***Falco peregrinus***	**Ubr**	
Golden Oriole	***Oriolus oriolus***	**Rm**	
Brown Shrike†	***Lanius cristatus***	**V**	
Red-backed Shrike	***Lanius collurio***	**Um**	
Lesser Grey Shrike†	***Lanius minor***	**V**	
Great Grey Shrike	***Lanius excubitor***	**Sm/Sw**	
Southern Grey Shrike†	***Lanius meridionalis***	**V**	
Woodchat Shrike	***Lanius senator***	**V**	
Magpie	***Pica pica***	**Cbr**	
Jay	***Garrulus glandarius***	**Ubr**	
Nutcracker †	***Nucifraga caryocatactes***	**V**	
Jackdaw	***Corvus monedula***	**Cbr**	
Rook	***Corvus frugilegus***	**Cbr**	
Carrion Crow	***Corvus corone***	**Cbr**	
Hooded Crow	***Corvus cornix***	**Ubr**	
Raven	***Corvus corax***	**Ubr**	
Goldcrest	***Regulus regulus***	**Cbr/Cm/Cw**	
Firecrest	***Regulus ignicapilla***	**Rm**	
Blue Tit	***Cyanistes caeruleus***	**Cbr**	
Great Tit	***Parus major***	**Cbr**	
Crested Tit	***Lophophanes cristatus***	**V**	
Coal Tit	***Periparus ater***	**Cbr**	
Willow Tit	***Poecile montana***	**V**	
Bearded Tit	***Panurus biarmicus***	**Sbr/Rm**	
Short-toed Lark	***Calandrella brachydactyla***	**V**	
Woodlark	***Lullula arborea***	**V**	
Skylark	***Alauda arvensis***	**Cbr/Cm/Cw**	
Shore Lark	***Eremophila alpestris***	**Rm/Rw**	
Sand Martin	***Riparia riparia***	**Cbm/Cm**	
Swallow	***Hirundo rustica***	**Cbm/Cm**	
House Martin	***Delichon urbicum***	**Cbm/Cm**	
Red-rumped Swallow	***Cecropis daurica***	**V**	
Long-tailed Tit	***Aegithalos caudatus***	**Cbr**	
Greenish Warbler	***Phylloscopus trochiloides***	**Rm**	
Arctic Warbler†	***Phylloscopus borealis***	**V**	
Pallas's Warbler	***Phylloscopus proregulus***	**Rm**	
Yellow-browed Warbler	***Phylloscopus inornatus***	**Um**	

Bird Index

K

L

M

O

P

R

S

T